BASKETBALL COACHING PRINCIPLES

Manuel Narvaez

Author

"Never let fundamentals and building skills take a backseat to game planning. Game plans win games. Fundamentals win championships."

(Thomas Crean)

FOREWORD

I have had the good fortune and pleasure of knowing Manuel Narváez for many years, beginning with his collegiate and early days as a professional player, followed by his years as an accomplished athlete and member of team Puerto Rico, to finally becoming a role player in the latter part of his career. Throughout this time, there has been one constant: Manuel has been a lifelong student of the game of basketball. While on the court setting a screen for his teammate to sink the buzzer-beater, grabbing a crucial rebound, or scoring inside the paint, he was always attentive to learning from his coaches and other players how to improve his own game and best contribute to the overall performance of his team. As a seasoned veteran, he became a mentor to the next generation of players by teaching them these hoops fundamentals. Following his retirement in 2015, he has done the same with countless adolescents.

In his second basketball book, Basketball Coaching Principles, Manuel takes his basketball teachings to another level. His focus now is to teach coaches how to be successful in developing players and future coaches. What is perhaps most special about his basketball coaching lessons is that the same transfer to life off the court. Not every player (myself included) will excel at the high school or collegiate levels.

More so at the pro level. Yet, successful coaches will prepare every player to succeed in life, given that the fundamentals imparted in the game relate to everyday situations.

Discipline, team play, practice, learning to win and lose, as well as leadership, are some of those core values. In my own non-sport profession, those consequential teachings made me the individual I am today. They are also the lessons that I impart to the members of my work team in coaching them how to, in turn, teach others to be successful in life. Basketball Coaching Principles is a reminder that we can all be excellent coaches on and off the court.

Gustavo A. Gelpí
United States Court of Appeals Judge and lifelong basketball aficionado

Basketball Coaching Principles

Why did I write this book?

In my first book, called *The Meaning of Basketball in Life*, I explain the importance of basketball by proposing a series of life skills values that I learned from basketball and could apply the concepts in daily life. This time, I want to take the concepts about basketball I learned from many coaches worldwide to propose a safe coaching model. This model will increase the chances of using basketball to develop players and coaches to form their professional careers successfully. Coaches need a mentor who can guide them and inspire them to make their dreams come true while being the coach players deserve.

The book proposes a mindset that will help the new generation of coaches and student-athletes to experience the total capacity of a functional basketball experience. More importantly, the mindset will also enable them to have a great relationship with the sport. The concepts and teaching methodologies apply to sports in general. Unfortunately, there are many misconceptions about coaching and training in today's basketball era. The essence of basketball has been diluted and distorted by what is popular and marketable. Many coaches, parents, and players are left disappointed and opt to withdraw.

It's unfortunate that many talented student-athletes are misguided and led down a path towards failure, often never reaching their full potential. The Basketball Coaching Principles offer a unique approach by incorporating Lean Management principles to improve efficiency and The Art of War strategies to help develop effective execution strategies.

This book aims to inspire coaches to question their methods and become the best possible version of themselves. By teaching life skills and techniques, coaches can help student-athletes succeed both on and off the court. I hope this book serves as a guide to help coaches become the best version of themselves and empower student-athletes to reach their full potential through the life skills and techniques taught.

TABLE OF CONTENTS

BASKETBALL COACHING PRINCIPLES

INDICATOR I: UNDERSTANDING OWN PHILOSOPHY AND BEING AWARE OF THE RESOURCES

TACTICAL QUESTION: WHAT WILL THE COACH LOOK FOR WHEN COACHING A TEAM AND ESTABLISHING PRINCIPLES?

INDICATOR II: ORGANIZATION, PRACTICE STRUCTURE, AND PLAN

TACTICAL QUESTION: WHAT WILL THE COACH DO TO MAXIMIZE THE PLAYERS' POTENTIAL AND HAVE THE TEAM PERFORM AT PEAK EFFICIENCY?

INDICATOR III: LEARNING AND ENJOYING GOES MANO-A-MANO

TACTICAL QUESTION: HOW WILL THE COACH ENSURE THE PLAYERS LEARN, ENJOY, AND SUCCEED?

OFFENSIVE PRINCIPLES

INDICATOR IV: DECISION-MAKING AND AWARENESS

TACTICAL QUESTION: HOW CAN THE PLAYERS MAKE EFFECTIVE DECISIONS AND MINIMIZE RISKS?

INDICATOR V: OFFENSIVE PROTECTION: THE COACH WILL ENSURE TO HAVE SOLID OFFENSIVE BALANCE AND SAFETY OUTLETS ADAPTABLE TO DIFFERENT GAME SITUATIONS

TACTICAL QUESTION: WHAT WILL THE COACH DO TO COUNTER-ATTACK DIFFICULT SITUATIONS AGAINST AN OPPONENT WITH MORE ADVANTAGES?

INDICATOR VI: UNDERSTANDING DIFFERENT OFFENSIVE OPPORTUNITIES, DEFENSIVE WEAKNESSES, AND ATTACKING THEM CONSTANTLY

TACTICAL QUESTION: HOW CAN THE COACH ANTICIPATE DIFFICULTIES, USE THE ELEMENT OF SURPRISE AND PREPARE THE TEAM TO SUCCEED?

DEFENSIVE PRINCIPLES

INDICATOR VII: A COACH STRESSES POSTURE, ATHLETIC STANCE, AND DEFENSIVE BEST PRACTICES

TACTICAL QUESTION: WHAT WILL THE COACH DO TO PREVENT DELAYED CLOSEOUTS AND MISMATCHES?

INDICATOR VIII: THE COACH MUST HAVE SOME EXPECTATIONS WHEN DEALING WITH TRANSITIONS, FAST BREAKS AND QUICK HITTERS

TACTICAL QUESTION: WHAT RULES APPLY IN MOST SITUATIONS AGAINST A FAST AND AGGRESSIVE TEAM?

INDICATOR IX: PROACTIVE DEFENSE, SETTING TRAPS, AND ROTATIONS

TACTICAL QUESTION: HOW CAN THE COACH HAVE A PROACTIVE AND AGGRESSIVE DEFENSE AND PROTECT AGAINST AN ADVERSE SITUATION?

C⬤ACHING

PR⬤NCIPLES

*"Basketball is one of those rare opportunities where
you can make a difference, not only for yourself but
also for other people."*

(William Theodore 'Bill' Walton III)

TACTICAL QUESTION: WHAT WILL THE COACH LOOK FOR WHEN COACHING A TEAM AND ESTABLISHING PRINCIPLES?

PRINCIPLE 1: Coach's philosophy

PRINCIPLE 2: Easy and simple, efficient and effective

PRINCIPLE 3: Set plays dilemma

PRINCIPLE 4: Alignments and spacing

PRINCIPLE 5: Matchups and individual skills

PRINCIPLE 1: COACH'S PHILOSOPHY

When coaching a team, you must ask several simple questions: What are my general coaching beliefs? What am I looking for offensively and defensively? What am I excellent in and passionate about in coaching and developing? What is the age group I am addressing? To whom can I compare my ideals? These relevant questions that will guide your thought process in your coaching journey.

We all know you will succeed in teaching if you master a subject. You must become a student of the game and strengthen your coaching capabilities. You must also understand that your coaching philosophy will take years to develop.

Your coaching philosophy will be established based on your own experience, whether as a former player or the close interaction and relationship with players and coaches. Constructing your philosophy will be led by the resources, your understanding of the best practices of basketball, and what you believe will address the needs of the players. Your resources can be your coaching notes from a conversation with successful coaches, coaches' video clinics, reading articles, training, or even mentorship. Seek for a moment those admirable qualities from coaches that you will want to apply in your coaching career. Identify the traits of the coach you want to be.

Once you know the resources, you will establish your philosophy and dedicate time and effort to reconstruct them into a system. Your philosophy will distinguish you from the others and will be your point of guidance. You will focus practices and drills on that subject you believe in and master. Once you are confident in what you believe in, you will also feel confident and capable of assessing the team's characteristics you are coaching. You will be able to modify instruction, strategy, and tactics that best fit your group and individuals.

Always ensure that what you teach is safe and prudent for the age and skill level you are coaching. Here are some examples of coaching philosophies based on offense and defense:

OFFENSIVE PHILOSOPHIES

○ Fast break oriented. Often seeks to push the ball ahead, not giving the defense a chance to set up.
○ Controlled game. Make more interventions and may focus on roles.
○ Deliberate game. Let the player make more deliberate decisions with less intervention from the coach.
○ Half-court oriented. Seeks to maximize possessions and the use of the shot clock.
○ Inside (down-load) game. Seeks to play from the inside out by giving more touches to the posts and creating the situation for it.
○ Perimeter oriented. Develop most of the play for the shooters.

DEFENSIVE PHILOSOPHIES

- Pressuring team. It can be full or half-court pressure to force the offense to turn the ball over or change directions constantly to affect their spacing and block driving and passing lanes.
- Zone defensive team. It intends to protect different areas of the court based on the offensive's strengths.
- Man-to-man defense. Focus more on matchups and individual skills to contain multiple scoring-capable offensive players.
- Trapping team. It intends to force lob passes that are easier to steal by trapping one offensive player with two defensive players.

Knowing when you need to adjust your philosophy to meet the team's and professional needs to maximize your player's skills are essential. It is vital as a coach to be humble enough to be flexible in adjusting your ideals to benefit your team's characteristics and personalities. For example, you will encounter situations where you are not experiencing team chemistry, the offensive or defense seems too broken, and nothing seems to fix it. But then, you watch a team video tape and realize that your team has a particular strength that was not perceived instantly. You may see that, in general, the players' skills provoke a true game character that is not what you naturally observe. It wasn't also what you have planned, but you need to embrace it, modify, build on it, and use it to your advantage.

I heard the following in a coaches' clinic. "Coaches seek to set a few norms that can adapt to many situations. But there are exceptions. When there are a few exceptions, we can assimilate it.

When there are many exceptions, not everybody will adopt your idea, and new systems will be developing."

So, if you are trying to develop players and leave a legacy with your coaching career, make sure that your ideas are adaptable and straightforward enough so your student-athletes can assimilate them. Then, you will succeed in your coaching career.

PRINCIPLE 2: EASY AND SIMPLE, EFFICIENT AND EFFECTIVE

The coach is responsible for simplifying the game as much as possible, besides looking for tactics to execute during practice and games. In that quest, one of the main object-ives in basketball, besides trying to score an easy basket by maximizing opportunities and creating advantages on offense, is to simplify the defensive coverage by covering more space on the floor without losing the integrity of the defensive triangles. The defensive triangle is the stance that allows a player to see the ball and man, which puts the player in an efficient help position.

We also seek to reduce the use of your players' resources, such as time, energy, and body risks. By doing this, you are creating an advantage for your team, offensively and defensively. In striving for that, we must ask ourselves the following questions:

○ How can I increase efficiency? First, it seeks how to reduce the waste of time and effort. For example, not being in a defensive triangular position inhibits the way to move in space faster and on time. Con-stantly improve and reduce waste, such as over-dribbling, shooting every time they are open, catching their players off-balance, forced isolations, and out-of-position shots. It also seeks how you can help the players improve in strength and skills in other game areas.

○ How can I increase effectiveness? It seeks to maximize opportunities, accuracy, and generate advantages constantly, and how the strategy(s) can be executed easier, shorter, and less risky. The tactic seeks a way to execute that doesn't hurt. It also strives to minimize the risks and harm, making it easier to remediate and turn into a counter-attack.

○ How can I teach drills and tactics in a simplified way, progressively and logically? It seeks to unpack or break it down systematically into digestible pieces and increase in difficulty once they progress during the established goals.

○ How do I do justice to my players? It seeks to determine how it will help the player who is not performing well and how I can allocate them to succeed instead of stigmatizing the player. This question is uncommon. The belief is that forcing players out of their comfort zone will make them winners and better players. By default, you ignore the player's multiple intelligences, needs, and realities, such as skills, ways of learning, body constitution, and psyche. Some players can improve by recognizing what is done right, and others can take constructive criticism more openly. Some other players can learn and execute by extreme force because it is what the player is undergoing to live through their development in the past. Sadly, they don't see any other option but to submit to whatever.

These are common questions that successful coaches may ask themselves. What is the most simple shot? What would your answer be? Remember, it seeks the most secured shot and higher percentage shot. Possible solution: an open layup, agreed? It is a fantastic way to start building the pieces. So this will generate another question: What is the most effective way of creating situations where my players can get open driving and passing lanes for an open layup? Possible answer: creating <u>disadvantages for the opponent</u>. Creating disadvantages increases the chances for easy layups or higher percentage shots. So the next question will be, how can I constantly force disadvantages to the opponent?

Now you are building a foundation by formulating the right questions. You will find the answer to this question in the following indicators.

When we are taught about basketball, we need to visualize it to comprehend it. We may be playing or being in the field as observers, but that helps us put pieces together while learning new things. If you didn't have the chance to play basketball and want to coach, you need to find an experienced coach. Watch their practices or be a volunteer assistant to help you build a coaching foundation.

We, as coaches, have to think about the best ways of doing things. So it is why you ask the 'layup question.' But things are not that simple. Too many variables make it difficult to have easy layups, then move to the following and most effective and efficient way to score a basket.

Think the same way defensively, but the questions will change. You may formulate the question; how do I want my players to play defense? If the opponent is not an outside threat: Do you want to play zone to give them a chance to rest and save energy while protecting the paint? Do I want players on the weak side close to their players and weaken the middle? Can they have their back turned to the ball in denial, or do I want them to be in a defensive triangular stance where they can see it? What would your answer be?

Later, after reading these principles, you will compare and contrast what you already know with possible new information. You will be amazed at what you knew but forgot to realize until now! Then, you can construct your coaching philosophy based on something other than what is currently popular. (Right now, handles and long-range shots are famous. It will end, the 'retro' will come again, and we will value traditional big men and point guards). This fever might not disappear for a while, but you want to build your team on solid and durable principles.

PRINCIPLE 3: SET PLAYS DILEMMA

Many coaches believe that you need a long list of set plays, and continuations give the illusion you are working the right way. How often do you see a set play at a youth level? You may wonder why it is too difficult to run a set play. But, it is not surprising that many coaches want to run set plays before even breaking the half-court extended pressure. Extended pressuring teams disrupts offensive patterns or pathways and makes it difficult to run them.

Ask yourself: When do I need set plays? Set plays are an essential part of the basketball structure. It gives a player or team a sense of direction, but the problem is that it lasts a couple of attempts, and that's it. After that, they might need more plays to run, especially when facing a pressuring team.

Several offenses can be used as templates to teach players how to read the game, adjust their mindset, and react. For example, you can use the five-out motion, the flex offense, and the triangle offense using the 1-4 formation to teach basketball fundamentals. With these templates, you can teach principles such as pass, cut thru away and replace, flare screens, backdoors cut, off-ball screens, zipper screens, and shallow cuts.

Once the fundamentals are taught properly, players can break the extended pressure more consistently without a set play and just by reading the game. And once set plays are in place, they can be creative when confronting different situations. But first, they must be taught the fundamentals to make set plays effective.

How many teams face the set play dilemma? First, your main shooters or guard players can't create situations or execute the play without breaking pressure. You will see forced shots from the shooting guards or most open shots taken from the role players. In basketball, at any level, if role players are not doing anything productive when they are off the ball, your guards players are pressured. In many instances, they are forced to pass the ball to the role player for an out-of-position shot.

Set plays are necessary, but before, the players must force the defense to retreat from their extended half-court pressure to make them <u>reactive.</u>

SET PLAY ILLUSION

I believe that set plays result from a good offense execution made by the players' creativity. But not a specific pattern given, but it was copied by a scouting coach to try to implement it in their team as a set play. Then, the elements used and conditions presented by the players that made that execution successful are implemented in an offense sequence and were given the name as a 'set to play.'

Behind the scenes of a set play, many principles interact. Still, most ignore them because many fans, players, and coaches are con-templating the apparent superficial beauty of the stage. The beauty relies on principles such as proper spacing, changes of speeds and rhythm, screen timing, movement fakes, handoffs, constant relocation, eye contact/signal, bounce passes, extra passes, and contact. If the players don't know or apply these principles, then the set plays 'never' will occur.

People often ignore coaches who value such principles and teach them. The popular YouTube training channels include visually impressive long-range shots and handles. These are part of basketball, but basketball is much more than that.

Don't fall into the trap of the set plays approach. Tons of salespeople online will make you believe that a successful play from a college is the answer you need. Think about it; there is much more than just a set play. What about the player's different creativity, team personality, and individual body strengths and experience level?

Coaches, make sure you teach your player great basketball principles before practicing any set play; they will save you a lot of time and effort.

PRINCIPLE 4: ALIGNMENTS AND SPACING

At the beginning of the game, coaches will seek to evaluate the opponent's alignment. They must analyze their spacing on that alignment, assess whether it is functional or dysfunctional, and find the strength and weaknesses.

You can tell how disciplined a team is by how they modify their defensive positioning to keep the integrity of the defensive alignment or, in the same way, its improper alignment. Another way is how they communicate if the alignment is missing an element, how they fix a misalignment relative to spacing and positioning or identify matchups in defense. Let me clarify positioning; finding their positioning is not just going to a spot designated by the coach and standing there, not at all. It recognizes your position and role based on your capabilities and strengths. This will help you to find your area of expertise within the overall alignment to make the offense or defense functional.

It is the moment that you assess if the opponent has basketball sense. It will help you set traps and take risks feeling confident they will struggle to identify the situation or recover on time on a defensive rotation.

There is not much need for set plays when teaching offense, especially to young players. Use just formations but teach them how to move when they are off the ball, one pass away from the ball, when two guys are close together, and when they are on the weak side. Formations can be aligning the offensive players oppo-site from the defense's alignment. For example, you can use 1-3-1, 1-2-2, 2-3, 3-2, and 2-1-2 formations as a counter positioning against the defensive alignment.

Teaching formations helps players to make initial plays, you don't have to stress in continuation at first, and they must get the idea and feel comfortable. Having them execute other options might be confusing. Have them run the initial formation and let them play by the principles of the game taught during practice. We must empower players, giving them the freedom of judgement to move and execute. They will make any initial play successful if they have mastered the principles guided by the coach during practice. Once they can under-stand to run the initial play, add continuation to complete the play and counter-attack the opponent's initial adjustment. Later on, I will share the offensive foundation that will help players how to move to most of the given situations and formations in offense alignments.

Going back on set plays, set plays take time and can be dis-rupted with simple variables. It is why players 'never' run the play, and it is time-consuming. We always blame the 'weak link' player for failing to execute the play. Somebody will always miss the play's timing for diverse reasons and if the principles are not appropriately indoctrinated.

It is why it is so necessary to assign roles, delineate responsi-bilities, and have players in their proper area playing on their strengths. Once they are clear of what is expected, you will be surprised how they add elements of creativity to a set play formation.

You may use a positionless offense-like motion if coaching in a recreational league. Let the players experiment with different positions for development purposes. Just make sure not to limit the experienced players. Experienced players may constantly be out of their place and lose confidence due to poor performance by playing in a 'non-structure' or 'non-competitive' environment.

Remember, it is not just about developing non-experienced players but successfully providing rigorous and challenging training to experienced and dedicated players.

PRINCIPLE 5: MATCHUPS AND INDIVIDUAL SKILLS

Besides the alignments, two more things that knowledgeable coaches seek when starting the game are the matchups and, subsequently, the individual strength and weaknesses of the opponent.

At the warmup, coaches should evaluate the opponent's players. Before the game starts, the players already know who their matchups in defense are. Once the game begins, the coach will assess the matchups, make adjustments, or identify some main weakness and attack it. For example, the coach will identify entry pass patterns, then will position their players in an advantage situation to deny the entry pass. In addition, the coach will continually assess individual skills such as players' weak hands, hot hands, shooters, energy level, low shooting percentage, and stagnating players during the game. Assessing matchups and individual skills will allow the coach to set some pressures, traps, or protect the team from dominant players.

INDIVIDUAL SKILLS

When working on skills development, you must make different assessments to test the player's previous knowledge.

Once you know what they know, you work on introducing basic drills and fundamentals to build that background basic knowledge that the player may be lacking. Next, you will introduce higher level and rigorous drills as new content to challenge them. At last, we must assess and provide feedback to fill any gap a player might have before moving to a more advanced stage of the player's development process.

Practices are the core of player development, but games are what is going to help the player to master specific skills. It is also imperative in open competitions. When your team has a substantial advantage, let your players work on their weaknesses more freely. For example, the big guy can dribble down, take outside shots, and the guard can post up.

To give a player a good training experience, we as coaches need to understand how the player learns. Players learn logically and progressively. You must break down the drills in a way they can digest. Then, you will add the pieces together and come to a stage where they will demand more rigorous activities.

Your team needs basketball fundamentals, and you must create game situation drills to help the players translate that into the game. An excellent way to help them execute the skills learned in the game is to add a challenge section after the drills have been taught. A challenge section is where the players compete in <u>Controlled Live Game Simulations (CLGS)</u>. It will boost the player's energy and motivation and avoid putting them to sleep by going over drills to drills.

I would highly recommend that the drills created must resemble a part of your continuation offense, either from a set play or motion offense. It is OK to implement set plays, as long it is done purposely, players know the principles, and they have progressed during the drills delivered in practice.

Indicator II: Organization, Practice Structure, and Plan

Tactical Question: What will the Coach do to maximize the players' potential and have the team perform at peak efficiency?

PRINCIPLE 6: Meaningful practice plan elements

PRINCIPLE 7: Metrics and parameters

PRINCIPLE 8: Teaching variation

PRINCIPLE 9: Organization and culture

PRINCIPLE 10: Basketball discipline

PRINCIPLE 11: Building habits

PRINCIPLE 12: Designating roles and responsibilities

PRINCIPLE 13: Team ground rules

PRINCIPLE 6: MEANINGFUL PRACTICE PLAN ELEMENTS

Coaches should include meaningful elements in the practice plan to give a sense of direction. Coaches must establish a timeframe for the expected end goal that the players must learn when creating practice plans for the pre-season. Once the end goal is selected, the coach designs a plan with the corresponding drills to help the players progress until the established goal is mastered. In the educational system, they call this strategy 'Backwards Design.' For example, the players are expected to make 75 layups in two minutes by the second week of practice as a team conditioning. Also, skill-wise, the players are expected in two weeks of beginning the pre-season to score 55% percent in static jump shots as a cool-down after practice.

With those expectations, as a result, the coach will focus their practice plans with drills to target those skills to master the expected goal. Once the two-week phase is complete, the coach will proceed with the corresponding plan established the same way. The coach then will subdivide the goals into objectives to target and teach them by progressions.

Progressions are just another way of continuity. Progressions challenge the players to move up in complexity once the expected knowledge is reached. The coach will gradually increase the player's independence by having fewer interventions. Once the goal is mastered, an increment in difficulty in the next stage or segment is necessary to push them to the next level of an advanced objective that will enable them to develop resilience.

Once the subject is introduced, the right practice time and a fair amount of repetitions are necessary to help increase skills and practical knowledge. The same principle applies to conditioning.

Conditioning is essential to a player's development as it prepares the body for the rigor the game demands. The conditioning section in a practice plan is also as necessary as the skills development and build-up section addressed in the following indicators. Coaches must have a practice plan for every practice section. Review the teaching points of the drills at least the day before to ensure that the objectives will be met and align with the established end goal.

PRACTICE PLAN AND STRUCTURE

I have developed a practice plan that divides the practices into four significant areas: Conditioning, Skills Development, Team Build up, and Game Simulation. These critical areas will include four progression levels and a challenge suggestion. You can create a practice plan format that better suits your needs or understanding, but I provide a practice plan template to use as a guide.

The practice plan contains essential elements supporting the four significant areas mentioned above and is divided and explained in Sections One and Two.

Practice Plan Template

BASKETBALL PRACTICE PLAN TEMPLATE

Practice Plan #	Time	Date	Season	Coach(s)
Primary Focus				
Secondary Focus				

Goal:_____
Reflection:_____
Today's Emphasis:_____

Team:_____
Starters:_____

Progrn. Levels	CONDITIONING (O&D) (*) SKILLS DEVELOPMENT		TEAM BUILD-UP (O&D) GAME SIMULATION	
L1				
L2				
L3				
L4 (**)				

Time:____(m) Break:____(m) Rating:____   Time:____(m) Break:____(m) Rating:____   Time:____(m) Break:____(m) Rating:____   Time:____(m) Break:____(m) Rating:__

REMINDERS	GAME VOCABULARY	PLAYS & SPECIAL SITUATIONS

STRENGTHS	ANALYSIS	WEAKNESSES
Offense: Defense:		Offense: Defense:

Self-Evaluation:_____ = ____

Assessment Rating Scale: 1: Need Improvement | 2. Progressing | 3: Executing | 4: Dominates
Progression Levels: Level 1: Mimic Static, Dynamic (No ball/w.ball) | Level 2: Dynamic/Counters (No ball/w.ball) | Level 3: Dynamic, Dummies/Counters | Level 4: Dynamic w/Defense Live
(*) Station/Circuit for Camps, Lessons & Clinics: Rookie | Starter | MVP | Pro
(**) Level 4: Challenge Level | Controlled Game | Group Dynamics | Live
REPORT:_____
_____
_____

Manuel Narvaez

Date

For team management purposes, a practice date is necessary. This is your evidence of what took place. In addition, this can be used as a growth measuring tool as it helps you notice the days it took your team/players to master specific objectives.

Practice Number

Having the account of the practice number, you can study how many practices took your team to meet the goal. You find trends in this and use them to improve your coaching methods.

Goal

The goal states what is expected and what preparation is necessary based on the date of the season. For example, say you are about to start your pre-season. Your goal will focus on conditioning, team cohesion, and adaptability to coaching philosophy. Then, you will set the time frame to see the goal met and prepare plans to concentrate on reaching the destination.

Primary Objective

You need to teach many things in basketball, but time is limited. You will need to set your parameters to be effective in teaching. We must prioritize and focus on correcting one thing without ignoring other important aspects of the game. When you teach something in basketball, it also has a double effect that will improve other areas, so first, have a primary objective.

Secondary Objective

Once you have a primary objective, then delineate what is secondary. For example, suppose you are working on breaking the press on offense as the primary focus and using dummy defense. You are also working on defense perse. Therefore, it can be a secondary point to your practice plan to include defensive elements as well before working on breaking the press and using defensive players.

Emphasis

Once you are clear on your primary and secondary focus, write down the emphasis. The emphasis seeks to remind the players to concentrate on specific scenarios or techniques to execute during an actual game according to the objectives and vocabulary needed for that particular practice session. You use teaching points and example methods while they are learning progressions. For example, if you are coaching between the first two weeks of the pre-season, you can tell the players to step into the shot by using 'two-time-rhythm' on the move to catch the ball and shoot. The two-time rhythm of stepping into the shot can be an example of coming from the corner and curling to the elbow of the free-throw line to receive the ball in a balanced receiving posture. Once the player curls in a receiving athletic stance simultaneously, the player will stretch the inner leg as 'one-time.' The outer portion follows hard as the 'two-time' to catch and shoot the ball in a balanced rhythm. That way, your teaching points of the situations are known and not lost in the practice segment.

Assistant coaches play an important role here; they must be aware of the emphasis and will ensure players are re-directed by stressing specifics such: as good stance, hands out, calling a name to pass, no chatting on the sidelines, and so on. You emphasize by evaluating previous practices and common problems of habit that need to be corrected constantly until the behavior is modified. Remember, we are seeking perfection in a fair and just manner.

Motivation and Fun

Basketball should be fun, and the main objective is to enjoy it. Unfortunately, sometimes we are caught in the competitiveness of the sport that we put pressure on the players. Let's try to initiate the practice with something fun or with a positive message; once their dopamine levels are high, they can learn more while having fun. You can start the practice session with a quote, success story, joke, or a fun drill. Don't forget to compliment players individually on their accomplishments; they will want to continue striving to improve.

Conditioning

This first area in the practice plan is the most important in basketball. Players who have played at a high level know the importance of conditioning: body strength, agility, flexibility, coordination, and balance. There is nothing wrong with wanting a conditioning section in your practice plan. However, it should not harm the players but help them perform well and reduce injury risks. As a coach, you will have the opportunity to give the players this experience, and they might not get it in other private or school teams. So don't deny this conditioning section to the players even if you have limited practice time.

Be mindful that you can use this section to reinforce your practice plan. Suppose today's focus is team defense. You may include a defensive conditioning drill that involves team coordination, communication, and speed. You can do that or focus on exercises; it is okay. Just make sure that the activities are appropriate and healthy.

You may want to learn more about contractions and tensions such as Concentric and Eccentric Contractions and Isometric and Isotonic Tensions. You may also like to learn more about the exercises to ensure you are using them correctly, such as Aerobic, Anaerobic, Pilates, and Plyometric. You can use the type of contraction and tension in various exercises to ensure that players build body strength from a solid foundation. Unfortunately, not everyone has the luxury of having a conditioning trainer.

After the drills, use some <u>Controlled Live Game Simulations (CLGS)</u> exercises before or after the break. These exercises help the players stay active with minimum recuperation time and prepare their minds for the worst game scenario.

Remember, mainly at the recreational level, you may have players with poor coordination skills and reflexes, even with diverse functional needs. You may want to plan for them and divide them into smaller groups. By differentiating, you can work conditioning without a ball to help the players focus on running through limited space (using cones), running backwards, and making sudden turns as progressions. This way, you reinforce their locomotor skills and improve their planes of motions with exercises that will help them keep their center of gravity (balance) while performing higher-level drills. Everything can be implemented by using progressions strategies. The end goal for the first two weeks of practice is that the player can dribble effectively throughout the cones without losing the ball and maybe without falling onto the floor.

Skills Development and Progressions

This section highlights the drills intended to improve individual skills. There are a vast number of resources over the internet for this section.

Just make sure to select the exercises appropriate for the maturity level of individuals. Not everybody on the team has the same maturity level. So you can divide them into groups by experience level, similar to camps and clinics. The experience levels are Rookie, Starter, MVP, and Pro. No group is affected; you can dedicate quality time to small groups and make corrections or interventions.

Those who are more advanced will need more challenging and rigorous drills. Those skills are intended to be translated into the next section of the practice plan, Team Buildup. Therefore, each drill segment will be accompanied by a 'Challenge.' The challenge can be after each drill component has been taught. Also, you may give the challenge to a small group, and the other group may go to take a break and repeat with the other group once they come from the break. This way, you are maximizing practice time.

Team Build-Up and Progressions

This section will integrate group dynamics, and they will execute team-related drills and game situations. It might start from 3v0, 3v3, 4v0, and 4v4. We can create different competitive exercises and Controlled Live Game Simulations (CLGS). It will help them apply the practical knowledge necessary to translate it into the game.

Game Simulation

This section contains various game scenarios, press breaks, full-court press, set plays, and inbound situations. It can finish with a scrimmage. First, ensure you use game simulation drills that recreate what will happen in the game. Then, add rules or difficulties to make it challenging and rigorous. Here, you will see some 'Controlled Live Game Simulations' (CLGS) rules.

Have the teams:

- Make ten to win
- Two misses layups and run
- Make three stops
- Use designated 6th man offense
- Use designated 6th man defense
- Miss two shots and switch team
- No dribble (Flat Ball) passing game
- Three dibbles and one shot
- Three possessions and switch
- Four ball reversals before shooting
- Big guys, three touches before the team shoots
- Six ball touches or passes
- Don't allow an offensive rebound
- First to make 11, but assists are one point, offensive rebound,

a steal, but a turnover takes one point away.

You can find thousands of creative ideas on the internet to make it more engaging and competitive. Ensure the rules are well explained and safe, and players have fun.

Drill Time

It is vital to set a timeframe for the drills. It will help you to get the most out of the sections. There is no law on how your practice time will be used. Make sure you are aware of the time, but if you are having a grand 'teaching moment,' use your extended time, then modify the other section's timing.

Attendance

Keeping track of the attendance will help you review the concepts taught to the missing players. You are lucky to have your entire roster to show to practice, and you often have to modify your plan for the lack of quorum. The coach will plan for this possibility and review the content of the previews practices helpful for the absent players.

Special Situations

There is a small section I recommend using dedicated to particular situations. These are situations that commonly occur at the game, and the coach will write them in the practice plan so as not to forget to put them into practice. The coach may call a timeout during practice, set a shot clock, and run the situations. Then the coach will evaluate and add variations to the situations. For example, let's look at an inbound sideline play. The defensive team will deny the ball to the point guard so that the O2 or O3 players will need to get open to receive the ball and start the play with a certain amount of seconds on the shot clock. It will prepare the coach to study the player's ability to execute and create plays, confident that the team can run without the assistance of the point guard.

Note/Reminders

There is always something you need to discuss with players, coaches, or parents. For example, there may be a discussion about coordinating a snack list after games or reminding players and parents that players must wear the practice jersey all the time during practices. Maybe the coach has an idea during training and makes a quick entry not to forget.

PRINCIPLE 7: METRICS AND PARAMETERS

This principle includes section two of the practice plan and structure. It summarizes the content that will help you make studies on the plan. I separated this into principle seven to help you better visualize how to use the practice plan and its elements.

SECTION TWO

In this principle, I describe a way to use metrics and set parameters that will help you provide a more individualized developmental experience to your players and the team. Therefore, you can select your stage when defining parameters. I usually use four sets of 'Maturity Level' and four steps of 'Developmental Progression Level.'

These stages help me focus on teaching points, review, correct, and increase difficulties throughout the drills. But if we do not have stages, it will be challenging to teach progressively, track progress, provide feedback, and develop habits and discipline.

The Maturity Level is a stage broken down into pieces to guide the players throughout the drill until the level of maturity in a rating scale is reached. The maturity level are: Need Improvement, Progressing, Executing, Dominates. Our target maturity level is level three, which is the Executing level. For example:

Maturity Level

1. Need Improvement
2. Progressing
3. <u>Executing</u>
4. Dominates

These levels are like a blueprint that tells the stage of your team, your teaching, and the players' performance. You can apply these stages in any drill and evaluate a player or team.

Coach Analysis and Self-Evaluation

These Maturity Levels are also for coaches' self-evaluation. The coach will use these stages to evaluate their teaching or coaching, reflect upon that, and improve for the next practice. Create a space on the practice plan to comment on your coaching. You can refer to it as the season progresses to compare and reflect on whether there has been any coaching improvement.

Development Progression Levels

The following progression practice plan includes four developmental level progression stages with difficulties. Setting parameters as a measurement tool is necessary to help you track progress and prepare practice plans.

Example of progression levels:

Level One: Mimic Static > | Dynamic > | No Ball > | w/Ball
Level Two: Dynamic > | Counters > | No Shooting > | Shooting
Level Three: Dynamic > | Dummies > | Shooting > | Counters
Level Four: Dynamic w/Defense Live > | Controlled > | Deliberate

These progressions will be used in each stage of the proposed practice plan template. You may apply the more convenient
method for your team, but this will help you. Remember, there are
four phases in the practice plan: Conditioning, Skill Development,
Team Buildup, and Game Simulation. Each section uses the proposed measurement tools to hold accountable and guide coaches to
learn and study the game. These levels are just a guide to help you
have a direction.

Mimic Static is a way the player will work stationary and rigid
and pretend they are shooting a ball or boxing out and rebounding.
It avoids any distraction that involves shooting with the ball as they
focus more on balance, technique, and mechanics.

Dynamic is a way to include a motion in any direction but
does not necessarily include shooting. At a later stage, the coach can
implement shooting, dummies (Soft Defense), and counters ("Contingency
Moves"). I do not recommend using dynamic and defense at first if
you work with dribbling, shooting mechanics, rebounding, and pivot-
ing. This will avoid diverting players' concentration and potential in-
cidents if they don't have the maturity to perform higher-level skills.

Challenge

Once the drills are introduced and players apply the intended exercises, we can add more vigorous activities, difficulties, or challenges to overcome. It is essential to engage them with competitiveness, which in the plan suggested is Level 4 (Dynamic with defense-live). It is crucial to practice the drills taught competitively and realistically.

Strength and Weakness

The coach will also reserve a space on the practice plan to comment on the team's defensive and offensive strengths and weaknesses. It all serves as a research tool for teams and self-improvement.

Coaching Points and Drills Description

The coach will prepare a plan for the upcoming practice(s). First, the coach needs to review the drills on the coaching board and write down essential details called 'coaching points.' Once the coach has this set and written down on the practice plan, they will share it with the assistant. The assistant coach will also share any drill suggestions.

Sample Coaching Points Review

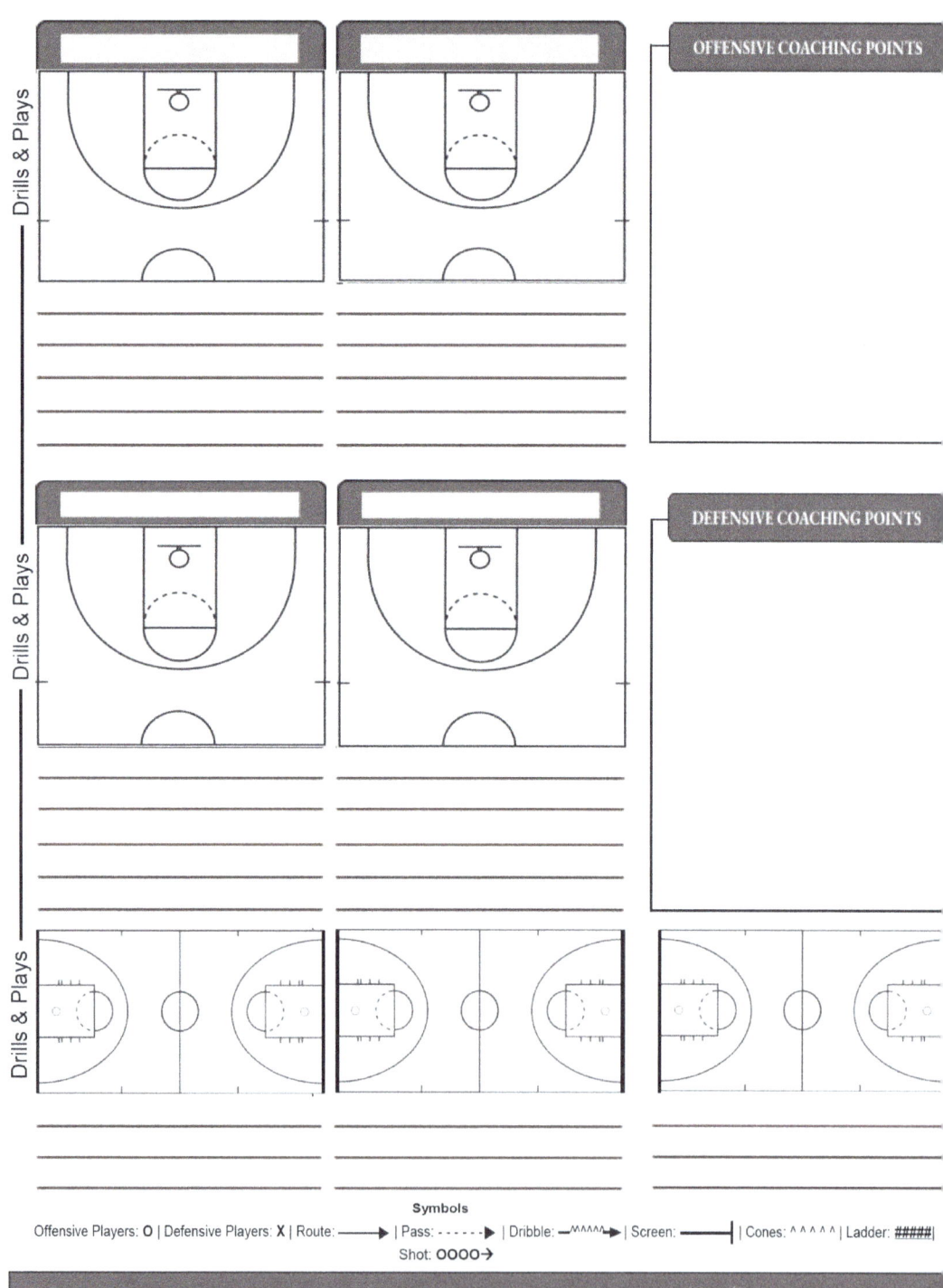

Drills & Plays

OFFENSIVE COACHING POINTS

Drills & Plays

DEFENSIVE COACHING POINTS

Drills & Plays

Symbols

Offensive Players: **O** | Defensive Players: **X** | Route: ⟶ | Pass: ┄┄▶ | Dribble: ⌁⌁⌁▶ | Screen: ⟶| | Cones: ^ ^ ^ ^ ^ | Ladder: #####|
Shot: OOOO→

Assistant Coach

Your assistant coach can make suggestions for your practice plan, share feedback on your coaching, explain the drills and demonstrate by selecting key players. The assistant coach also help by matching players in practice for any defensive drill or game simulations. In general, the assistant coach's role is to support the head coach and to have a proactive role guided by the head coach's parameters.

The head coach and assistant coach should have 'friendly debates.' When the assistant coach sees something in the game and wants to suggest it, the coach will ask why the assistant is considering it. The head coach might inquire more and explain the reason for disagreement. Suppose it sounds appropriate for the head coach, but it doesn't seem to follow what the coach is trying to do. Then the assistant, after some attempts, must continue to support the coach, and nothing changes.

The debate is essential to operate at peak efficiency. The assistant coach can't get discouraged and cease the suggestions because the head coach didn't use the suggestions in certain games. Remember, the coach has in mind a plan and a 'cause' which includes 'negotiating with some calculated risks.' The assistant might not be aware of the game situation presented, which means the assistant might disagree with the decision made by the coach at the moment. Still, the coach is taking a calculated risk that the assistant coach should respect.

Head coaches must be sensitive about what the assistant coaches are trying to share and be open to hearing something you may not agree with or dislike. In basketball, the relationship between coaches and assistants should be firm and filled with trust and honesty.

Assistant coaches' role is also to use different and unconventional self-made data collection methods ('stats') to help identify teams' offensive and defensive game trends. This will help target the areas of improvement of critical needs. The assistant coach should make recommendations to the coach based on the data collected. More information on this is found in principle 17.

Coaches can go online to find helpful information on delegating tasks to assistant coaches and the role of an assistant coach.

When practicing an individual skill or a drill that contains shooting, give the players at least five repetitions per drill; if not, they will only focus on scoring or missing. It will give them time to correct themselves and make adjustments. Coaches want them to focus on judgement and awareness. You focus on controlling the drills and their speed, then add variations as they progress. After appropriately teaching the 'drill,' let them make deliverate decisions and assess how they react. Give them room to solve the problem, and then you can make interventions progressively.

PRINCIPLE 8: TEACHING VARIATION

Your approach should vary based on whether you coach recreational or competitive basketball. For example, you don't have much time to practice and develop good habits in a recreational setting. Create a short routine with simple fundamentals such as posture in offense and defense. Then, engage them with different creative drills with meaning; they will learn fast while having fun.

After each drill execution progressively, it is advisable to have the student-athletes participate in 'Controlled Small Live Game Simulations' (CLGS). It is a way to make it rigorous and engaging. You control by making it challenging and setting goals or rules to be reached. This way, also you ensure they are engaged and not waiting too long to compete and to 'have fun,' which is the most fundamental principle in basketball. Players can be divided into positions and stations and work directly with specific skills with the 'inclusion objective' to have them performing with the general team's intended mastery goal.

You can vary the way you run your practice. For example, divide players by positions and work on skills relative to their roles or skills levels. Have them work with a partner with a similar maturity level or experience level.

Players can also work in a circuit by stations to work on different skills that may be out of their position. In addition, it allows them to work on their weaknesses.

The coach can also dedicate more time to using one of the four phases of the practice plan. For example, the coach commits most of the hour to Skills Development in practice and does the same with the other three practice plan phases based on the established goal.

Here is a list of some variations when assigning work to players or creating a practice plan:

- Specific skills group by positions
- Same maturity level group partners
- Different skills circuit stations
- Focus on conditioning
- Focus on skills development
- Focus on team build-up
- Focus on game simulations

This group dynamics will greatly help students-athletes with diverse functional needs and disabilities. It is imperative that you develop practice plans to modify the drills and change some rules to make them adaptable for these players. You will promote an inclusive environment. The idea will be to integrate these players as best as possible into the general group's objective and be able to add their value and experience to the team effort while enriching their lives.

PRINCIPLE 9: ORGANIZATION AND CULTURE

Players need to know what to expect, they want to have a sense of security, and they will compromise if the coach is transparent and organized in their teachings and drills. Players must have clear goals to put into practice and translate into the game. They will be able to do so if they are taught basketball discipline and good habits.

Players must be taught something to demand something from them in significant instances. For example, sometimes, a coach expects a player to relocate to the ball because it appears to be common sense. But, as much as it seems common sense, it is a discipline that coaches need to cultivate first.

Players will execute what they are taught repeatedly in practice logically and progressively. *As the players mature, coaches can strategically teach ideas or concepts with 'gaps' to challenge the athlete and allow them make the connection on their own. It will help players to be more self-sufficient and confident enough to master their capacity to apply their judgement in many game-like scenarios.* You do not need to provide everything in small digestible pieces. Again, it is just a manner of maturity that the coach will identify and tactically administer to them.

Coaches have their standards of processes so that when players get to the court, they know what to do. Have rules and enforce them; if not, there will be disorganization as soon as they walk into the gym or are on the sidelines.

Remember, you are the coach, be sensitive to what they say, but you can't have players debating with you or their parents in crucial moments. The coach will give student-athletes and parents a chance to discuss and express themselves in a planned open forum for team relationship-building. As much student-athletes need counseling and training, so do parents when it comes to understanding game and behavior expectancies. But the coach must ensure to have established objectives and rules. Post or share them as 'Acknowledgment form,' signed by parents and players on the first day of the pre-season meeting.

Critical: You can't teach or drill what makes sense to the players or the knowledgeable basketball stakeholders (parents, fans, owners, sponsors, leaders, and coaches). You teach what is going to make sense in the game and fix the long-term problem, even when it doesn't make sense initially, and your calculated risks create short-term disadvantages and controversies.

Observers may not see your intentions at a glance; later, the results will prove the point. Some things are not to be debated or non-negotiable. Coaches need to teach in the same structure and mindset and agree and coordinate before practice. The coach needs to be organized and have tasks delegated. Players must know what to expect. However, some things are unpredictable things. You need collaboration and trust to function as a team successfully.

Coaches and parents can't be deauthorizing other coaches and game officials with comments in front of the players, whether at home, driving to a practice or game, or on the site. The players will learn that and may rebel or boycott in diverse forms. However, coaches see this form of boycott daily in the manner of verbal statements, insubordination, body language, and lack of effort. This affects the general plan intended for all involved and creates an unhealthy atmosphere of disrespect for all parties present or related.

Acknowledgment Sheets

It is vital that the coaches create different acknowledgement forms, methods, and orientation sheets, which may include and are not limited to:

○ Parents' code of conduct and spectator expectations
○ Players' code of conduct and commitment to participate
○ Team ground rules
○ Protocols of coach's meeting requests and contact period
○ Do's and Don'ts when discussing matters with the coach
○ Do's and Don'ts of healthy conversations from parent to athletes before and after game
○ Different waivers of acknowledging risks
○ Nutritional consumption information
○ Sports safety information to remain injury-free during and after the season.

As coaches, we want to protect the athlete's integrity, dignity, and mental well-being and help them cope with social misconceptions regarding group acceptance and how sports are perceived. The forms instruct all people involved in sports' best practices to help us ensure student-athletes have a great relationship with the sport.

PRINCIPLE 10: BASKETBALL DISCIPLINE

What is basketball discipline? Basketball discipline is properly using techniques and teaching points when coaching basketball drills. It means that the coach will focus not only on behavior but also on the best practices of teaching technical points and demanding its application consistently until mastery. Examples are using proper posture in offence, hand usage, footwork in passing or stepping into the pass, proper v-cuts by setting up the 'defense,' and stepping into the shot. Of course, we need to exaggerate a little when showing the idea of the move, even if we look funny. The players need to understand the message and follow the coach's example.

It is important to exaggerate the moves until muscles get fatigued. In this way, players build 'muscle memory.' Not only focus on technique but awareness and judgement. If you have to remove the ball from the drill, do it. Combine what you are doing with how you are doing it. Like in karate, you don't only focus on technique but the spirit of it, meaning judgement and awareness.

Players can perform almost any move in offense, but we need to help them unlock it until it becomes familiar.

It is imperative to give the player a chance to practice a skill using different teaching variations and drills for a specific skill set in a measurable, logical, and progressive format. That way, they build discipline, unlock the move in the type of skills, and develop good consistent habits.

Habit building requires plenty of interventions and redirections. Still, once it is well addressed, it will become second nature in their subconscious, enabling them to activate the most accurate decisions in critical situations and conditions. Especially when the oxygen levels of the player are crucial or lacking, their instinct will help them execute, most likely accurately, based on the habit-building training endured by the player(s) in question.

PRINCIPLE 11: BUILDING HABITS

Coaches don't let the players get away with old habits that do not help increase the team's peak efficiency and effectiveness. Remember, you want patterns that will most likely increase the advantages for your team. Because a player might be the group star, don't let them get away with behavior that affects the team's harmony and game objectives.

For example, stress during practice that when players catch or even before they catch the ball, they must survey the court first instead of catching in transition and driving immediately. Another example is when they are about to rebound, they tend to see the shot and walk to the rim looking at the ball, and they have a tendency not to create contact or box out. Players must also be taught to land in perfect balance when rebounding or shooting a jump shot. This is a skill that needs to be reinforced. So, this is why the conditioning segment with the progression levels plays an essential role as it gives them time for the player to work on strength, coordination, balance, and rhythm.

They have old habits that need to be re-directed consistently. The coach will make interventions and correct these small details that can significantly disadvantage your team throughout the season.

PRINCIPLE 12: DESIGNATING ROLES AND RESPONSIBILITIES

Young student-athletes may not have the maturity to understand the concepts to be taught, or coaches may not have the time to prepare how they would like players to be. So instead, assign roles and describe their responsibilities, so that they can execute effectively and are part of the plan. They will most likely react by instinct once you give the functions and provide drills in different situations.

Players are on an assignment; when they are on the court and on the bench. You may ask yourself: What roles should be assigned, and why should it increase efficiency? What is the generally accepted practice in offense and defense at full and half-court? Who goes to stop the ball in transition, and who shouldn't? Who runs side to side relative to the ball? Who is the one-man fast break? In what situations can we put back an offensive rebound at the basket, and when can we reset? You must highlight these situations if your focus is winning in a competitive league or tournament. However, in a recreational league focused on development, the approach will vary for evident reasons.

In general, whoever is on the floor has an assignment or duty to perform, reaching for efficiency. Therefore, we must be cautious about establishing too many rules in different situations, and it's unrealistic to set expectations attached to too many regulations. We can teach more concepts and generally safe and accepted best practices based on successful data to help the team mature in their game.

If the coach wants order and control of the team, do justice to higher-skill and less mature players. Honor the time and effort of the stakeholders involved. Designate roles and delineate their responsibilities linked to the end goal expectations. Younger players can have freedom within an organized and structured system. As the players progress, you will give them more responsibilities, and your intervention may be reduced (scaffolding strategy). Still, they have to earn it and show the maturity to do so.

You give players an assignment, which is an opportunity for success. If you do not provide the structure, they will experience frustration.

CHAMPION'S MINDSET

I've been part of many teams and found how a champion's mind works. There is no magic, but there is a great <u>sense of urgency</u>. It all starts on the bench on how competitive they are with the regular team. Players from the bench have a role too. At a professional basketball level, not everyone can talk at the same time to players on the court. The coach should designate somebody of authority or confidence to approach the regular or starter players. Assign players who can approach the other to encourage or correct. Have them bring water to them and others to vent air and ignite the crowd. Coaches will enable them to take care of themselves outside of the court. They should be encouraged to rest and eat healthy, especially during playoffs. It is about efficiency, so the coach will counsel them on how to take care of themselves. For example, they can't sleep late because of playing video games, and there is a game the next day.

The coach will use the bench players finalizing the regular season to have them playing more and getting more shots to get those players with less playing time to stay in shape and rhythm. At a professional level, imported players need to know the culture. The coach should support them in coping with diversity and staying within respectful boundaries. The coach will have an assistant to support them. Every little detail counts. It makes the difference because an unhealthy relationship with society may affect their game.

Players with a champion mindset steps into the court, and they trust they can win, which translates into winning streaks. But the coach is educating them to be a champion. The players will sense if the coach seems stressed by the pressure of the playoff or the final game.

The coach is always preparing the team to be a champion. So don't change their routine abruptly during the playoff or in the championship game. Still, it is understandable to establish strict parameters.

Remember, it is not the championship that decides if you are a winner. It is the skills and life lessons learned throughout the season that you can apply in your life daily.

PRINCIPLE 13: TEAM GROUND RULES

The coach establishes team rules but lets the players also share insights. Letting the players share insights of team rules is helpful because they are more compromised when involved. But why is it important to establish ground rules? Because you will have to deal with diverse personalities and behaviors. You will have players there to experience the game of basketball (if it is a recreational league). They will, on occasions, distract others. You will also have to deal with different egos and bad habits from experienced players, and you will have some parents trying to coach from the sidelines.

Parents and players need to be educated about the best practices in a sports environment. Still, the coach also needs to model them. For example, players need to know that when you say 'ball,' they must stop. If they have a ball in their hands and you are speaking, they need to hold the ball and stop dribbling. They cannot be joking around or dancing. You need to set the respect and model it, not only because basketball is a privilege. You are helping them build character, but they are a distraction to others, and they will not honor everyone's time and the practice plan, of course.

It is a good way also to have parents on the sidelines supporting your discipline. When parents see players attentive and organized, it shows respect for the coach, and it will influence parents to do the same thing.

Being this the case, the coach will establish rules about basket-ball etiquette at the beginning of the pre-season. And the coach will have a system to hold the players accountable to either incentivise acceptable behavior, or correct negative behavior applying negative reinforcerment to discourage the behavior from reoccuring.

Here are some essential tips that are part of establishing team ground rules and disciplined team culture:

- Being on time
- Call if the player can't make it
- Proper language usage
- Don't talk when the coach is talking
- Appropriate dressing (shirts tucked in, etcetera)
- Remind them your rules constantly (written and verbally)
- Listen and respect the opinion of others
- Not sitting down when the coach is explaining
- At the whistle, everyone gathers immediately

The coach will be consistent in establishing rules and leading by example. Also, they will have a schedule ready available for parents and players. This all will give the player a sense of direction and security. *Please expect that the student-athletes will test your composure from time to time, but be patient; how you react will determine the extent of their respect.*

INDICATOR III: LEARNING AND ENJOYING GOES MANO-A-MANO

TACTICAL QUESTION: HOW WILL THE COACH ENSURE THE PLAYERS LEARN, ENJOY, AND SUCCEED?

PRINCIPLE 14: Engaging players during practice and warm-ups

PRINCIPLE 15: Diverse and fun

PRINCIPLE 16: A coach is a learning machine

PRINCIPLE 17: Coaching board, preparation, and stats

PRINCIPLE 18: Allocate players where they can be successful

PRINCIPLE 19: Functional or dysfunctional basketball system

PRINCIPLE 20: Coping with losses and preparing for the next game

PRINCIPLE 21: Coaches' locker room mysteries

PRINCIPLE 14: ENGAGING PLAYERS DURING PRACTICE AND WARM-UPS

Suppose the coach works in a small group, or the emphasis is a 1v1 situation. The coach's attention can't be divided. Instead of having the rest of the players waiting in line, have them execute another drill that doesn't require much of your attention. The assistant coach or volunteer can lead this and then rotate.

During warmups in practice or the game, give players a routine or a series of drills to keep them engaged and improve in game-like scenarios; if not, they will shoot long-range shots. Again, have your assistant lead this while focusing on other things, such as revising notes, roster, and scouting the opposite team.

Give them tasks with your assistant coach in small groups while you talk to parents about an issue. If you are reviewing a coaching point with your assistant, plan to have a parent/volunteer assist you. Never turn your back on players for safety reasons. It will also motivate parents being a part in their learning process and foster parents' involvement; they will appreciate it and help you. Assign players with drills intended to improve weaknesses while you manage some other stuff when you are against the clock. Have team leaders assist you with this as well.

PRINCIPLE 15: DIVERSE AND FUN

Ensure to begin practices with fun games or change how you start them creatively. Players will learn more when their energy levels are high. When players have fun, they have a higher level of engagement. They can concentrate more and will strive to improve their game.

If you see them getting sleepy when teaching fundamentals, diversify a little. Have them run or play competitive fun games before giving fundamentals instructions. Seek different ways to make them stay active; if not, it will be hard to stay focused. They may look around and not honor your time and effort.

From time to time, players need to be paying attention by waiting in line to see what others are doing. They can learn from mistakes or excellent example from peers. Alternatively, they can listen to your corrections to understand and execute properly and minimize interventions when they have their turn. Having them waiting and watching is OK as long as it is not a constant.

You have the right to combine. Don't forget to stop after certain training sections and make a fun and demanding game. This will engage them, and they will be excited and energetic when resuming your practice plan. Also, it is a tactic that will redirect their attention without giving them a long speech, which we must avoid.

PRINCIPLE 16: A COACH IS A LEARNING MACHINE

Coaches have many roles. It is why coaches need to study the game and seek improvement constantly. We must ask questions, dig deeper, invite a coach or friend to watch a game, and have a basketball conversation. So often, coaches are afraid sound like they are ignorant of the subject. Don't feel bad; every coach bases their focus on their philosophy, and they will see it from a different perspective. It is what makes you unique.

Coaches have many responsibilities and are under rigorous scrutiny always. There is a lot of competition, and many coaching proposals are being proposed while you are coaching. Coaches must schedule conferences to meet with parents and learn from their feedback, administrators, and other coaches. It would help if you created a network or association to advocate for coaches and share resources about coaching best practices. Coaches must meet and discuss, develop drills, use the coaching board to practice teaching points, and build practice plans. However, they must agree and teach the same generally accepted guiding principles.

We cannot afford to have coaches and assistant coaches explaining drills and teaching differently. This will confuse the player. Likewise, coaches cannot have parents dictating instructions from the sidelines.

COACH AS TRAINER

Conditioning is an essential part of the game, and many organizations don't have trainers certified to work with the teams. Although coaches serve as trainers, they must understand crucial body functions to suggest food consumption and provide resources and exercises. Coaches need to find information on different types of muscle tension, contractions, and planes of motion helpful to build practice plans and understand the appropriate biomechanics of the intended drill, especially the conditioning section. Also, they need to know their limitations in the field and not submit players to unmeasured and extreme exercises.

COACH AS TEACHER

Coaches seek ways to improve teaching and adjusting to ensure his/her players are learning. Coaches can read and subscribe to online salespeople in sports to get tips every day from articles they might share from experienced coaches. Coaches can also watch college women's basketball to learn the discipline and dedication in offense and defense and take notes on setting expectations for their team. You can take notes on what you see from players and hear from analysts. It is an excellent way to compare and contrast your opinion.

The coach can have an assistant that helps them with feedback on their teaching. Feedback is essential, and we need that to adjust instruction and practice plans. Don't stress yourself on many drills and plays; keep it a few. Have them repeat until the goal is met and move on. Players need to have fun, so reward them with exciting dynamics.

Don't feel pressured to find many creative and fabulous drills because they may be fun and give the illusion that they are helpful and appropriate. Too much creativity can distract players. Constantly changing the exercises for a 'creative one,' even if for the same intended skill, doesn't ensure they are learning and improving. For example, many handle drills may be fun. However, unless you explain the dribbling mechanics well and teach and reinforce the concepts and objective of dribbling well, you are not maximizing time and resources.

There are two main avenues to teach 'handles.' I prefer to call it dribbling, and I take avenue number two. However, it is not the only one. There are some misconceptions regarding this topic that I want to clarify. It is not intended to harm or minimize anybody.

Dribbling Avenues

Learning Avenue One: The player must bounce the ball at least 500 times a week for three months. In other words, the player needs to do 6,000 bounces to see improvements. However, suppose you add to those bounces different creative/fun drills. Then, the focus on a specific ball-handling target objective is lost, and concentration is divided. The result will be difficult to measure or establish, and progress will be difficult to follow and target particular weaknesses.

You will have to double or triple your bounce repetitions per three months for each new creative drill a coach provides for the player(s). It means a coach is extending the working plan year-round and increasing difficulties to experiment with slight improvement. In the process, many resources have been invested, such as time, effort and money.

Learning Avenue Two:

- Use fewer but engaging drills but focus on dribbling mechanics.
- Connect it with footwork.
- Synchronize these two with speed changes, contact, and offensive protection tactics. This will help with the general objective

of improving the passing angle for an on-time pass (1), breaking one-on-one pressure (2), and increasing the advantage to attack to the basket (3) to have more apparent passing lanes, which are the three most essentials principles of dribbling.

Once they master the proper mechanics and connect it with the dribbling concepts, the 'bouncing' repetition is less, and improvement is measurable and effective in less than three months. Players will have great quantifiable results. They will meet the target objective. Also, the end goal intended to master the game-like scenarios of dribbling skills required in-game, will be satisfied effectively and efficiently. Remember, bouncing the ball too much during the game kills the efficiency and timing rhythm of the team's offense.

COACH AS MENTOR

The coach teaches skills and values of basketball applicable to life, not just focusing on winning championships. There is more to basketball than that. Not everybody will win as they dream, but they can still be winners.

When speaking about teaching principles, we cannot take the values of teaching basketball for granted. All the perfect posture and mechanics we need to stress come with a life value and a lesson that will last forever. Coaches are a significant influence in the players' life. They don't only focus on winning but on empowering them to succeed in all aspects of life possible.

Coaches, keep contact with players. Send them or the parents a message from time to time or meet with them. You will be amazed at the added value. It will also motivate you and benefit your current players.

COACH AS MOTIVATIONAL SPEAKER

Many players experience frustration when they can't execute a drill properly or can't perform as expected. We must use the right words to encourage them, not put them down, and be prepared to use words of encouragement from practice to practice and game after game. Read books and seek messages that empower you to become a role model to the players. They are susceptible to what coaches speak. This is why coaches need to build relationships with the parents so they can tell you what is happening in the player's mind.

REFLECTING ON COACHING

Evaluate other coaches on how they teach, don't steal their style; do a reflection on what they are doing that makes them successful and make the necessary adjustment. Many coaches teach what they see, and replicate attitudes from others. Many personality traits are copied from coaches to coaches that don't do justice to the game or players, but it gives some coaches the illusion they are doing the right thing. Reflect on that, and ask yourself whether it benefits the player or hurts them. If you don't see an improvement from the player, don't blame them; look inside yourself and ensure you are original. Remember, many well ex-ecuted plays result from small, constructed details that require discipline. Know that many successful plays result from calculated measures and a lot of practice. The coach will break down the drills to their component level and build them until the final play is made. Then, the coach will rank their teaching of the subject and make notes on the practice plan reflecting on what worked out and what needs improvement. Again, you can use the scale provided for players on the practice plan and structure.

PRINCIPLE 17: COACHING BOARD, PREPARATION, AND STATS

During practice, the coach needs to show the players the alignments of the drills and the offensive and defensive formation on their coaching board before sending them to their assigned area. This will save a lot of energy for the coach when explaining the drill. It also teaches the players how to follow the drawings and make suggestions, which is necessary during games.

We can use technology to our advantage when we are teaching the players. For example, we can use an electronic board to record a player's movement. This resource is also exciting for them because you can write their names on the 'player's icon' on the board. Show them how you expect them to move, help, and cut. You can give them at practice the opportunity to draw what you just explained; it will help them focus, have more awareness of what they are doing, and have more fun while learning.

You may assign workouts at home and give them a list of drills and a link to watch a video of the exercises. Then, they will work with their parents and write the results and a brief reflection so you can track progress.

The coach is a catalyst for success for the player, and the coach needs to give them as many great experiences as possible. We are impacting them, and the best practices will prepare them to apply that outside the basketball court.

PREPARATION

The coach needs a binder with rules, game plans, and plays to review before the game. Coaches can include substitution charts and specific characteristics that distinguish each alignment, such as having a pressing squad ready to be assigned to the game. It is something that begins with planning and testing it in practice. Having a game plan helps you access this chart to face special situations. Coaches must practice special situations with players that will also serve as a teaching practice for the coach.

'UNCONVENTIONAL' STATS

Another essential element is stats keeping but in a different form and proactive. Your assistant coach or a volunteer can collect the information on a printed, self-made form. A coach can create a data collection form to help with in-depth deflections/turnover comparison, which is a must in youth leagues. Although this is where the team loses a lot of possesions or quality shots, it also helps coaches identify timing and spacing. How late are players arriving at the offensive player in a closeout? How reactive are they? It helps to reflect on how late they pass the ball and how stagnant the receiver is meeting it. It can be a form of quick data entry with a simple bubble marking to highlight the situation related to the turnover.

Using a self-made stats form, you can reflect when you broke the press when your players arrived on defense on time and compare results. Coaches will be amazed by the trends they can draw from this and improve their coaching, or at least, this will alert you about things you must focus on in practices.

Unconventional stats can significantly reveal where the players are underperforming and are not commonly highlighted in standard game statistics forms. For example, to have a stat of turnovers targeted and related to specific diverse passes as adverse situations on deflections, getting open, driving angle, and timing-reaction. You can compare and contrast the results with the intended goal and parameters. You will have the formula indicating the problem and suggest an appropriate solution to administer an adequate intervention.

Assistant coaches can collect many tangible and intangible stats to support coaches. The coach will gain tremendous knowledge, helping him/her to prepare practice plans and make successful corrections. In addition, it is an excellent way to develop players more precisely and take pressure away from players. Coaches will mainly identify things to self-improve, which will benefit parties involved.

PRINCIPLE 18: ALLOCATE PLAYERS WHERE THEY CAN BE SUCCESSFUL

A coach should maximize a player's potential and have players where they can succeed. We just don't bench players because they do not fit our philosophy. Players need to have the opportunity to express their skills and talents, and we must create a conducive environment for that. In a professional setting, you need to do what it takes to win, and you will play players that you see fit, and the others are benched, hoping to trade them. I do not sympathize with this, but at least these players get paid for that.

Youth league and college level should not be this way. We are educators. And we must seek ways to get the message across. We must understand their immediate needs and be facilitators for them to succeed. We can begin by being aware of their personal goals and needs. Then, we have to make sure it aligns together.

Players at a professional level are afraid to lose what constitutes security, their source of income, and job security. For youth, it is a matter of playing time and securing a spot on the team. If that is not taken care of, it is when it comes to the individual game. Then begins the anarchy in your group. Instead, assess their strengths and weaknesses thoroughly, allocate them to situations they can perform, and give them the freedom to make mistakes.

Delineate to the player's reachable and vigorous targets/objectives to reach. Once they show progress, then take a moment to speak about the accomplishments and improvements as a team and individuals. Sit on the court and tell them things you see in them and have improved. Celebrate their success! It is the beauty of basketball and coaching when setting measurable and realistic objectives. You allow players to find themselves valuable to the team by helping them have small accomplishments, which increases morale, self-esteem, and confidence level in their game. Still, they will also consider themselves as 'winners' no matter if the championship is won.

Remember, players get tired of being told the wrong things. So give them tangible or intangible rewards such as certificates, medals, trophies, and praise. Positive reinforcements come in different attributes. It can be a tangible reinforcement, edible, sensory, and activity reinforcer such as 'fun time.'

PRINCIPLE 19: FUNCTIONAL OR DYSFUNCTIONAL BASKETBALL SYSTEM

When coaches use different measuring tools, they note reflection, target objectives met according to scale, shooting percentage, deflection against your team, and turnovers. You can identify traits in your system that 'scream' whether you have a functional or dysfunctional system.

Based on this, you can set priorities in preparing practice plans and emphasize correcting the issues. At practice, we need to focus on drills that will help us fix those problems early on in the game. Not just creative and entertaining exercises to improve basketball skills like dribbling, passing, and shooting, but drills presented in a game-like fashion and simulating its intensity. Below are some significant dysfunctional basketball offense and defense 'characteristics.'

DYSFUNCTIONAL OFFENSE

- Inbounding the ball and leaving behind the ball handler
- Catching and dribbling right away
- One pass and a shot
- Dribbling only to the right side
- Dribbling to the side with the opposite hands

- Standing straight to receive the ball
- Waiting for the ball in one spot
- Trying to split three defenders with no momentum
- One offensive rebound and a forced shot
- Passing late while dribbling fast and colliding with the defender
- Stagnate reaction while watching your teammate getting trapped while protecting the ball
- Two or more guys wanting to meet the ball, bringing defenders to trap and forcing lob passes
- Driving full-court through long open side lanes
- Escorting the guard at a higher speed and leaving them far behind
- No ball reversals
- No skip passes
- No drives and dish close to the basket
- No dribble drives and kick-outs
- Jumping on closeouts

DYSFUNCTIONAL DEFENSE

- After a shot, guards don't watch the defensive balance
- In the transition to defense, trying to stop a player by two or more players chasing the ball
- Stagnate, reactive, passive, or lazy defense
- Not denying passing lanes or entry passes
- Not being in an athletic stance
- Not flying to their man when the ball is released
- Reaching in to steal the ball
- Gambling and reaching-in in transition to defense after a turnover

- ○ Not creating contact with whoever comes across the paint
- ○ Not pushing out to the weak side, the middle cutter
- ○ Not denying ¾ the post-passing lane
- ○ Not stunting in dribble-drives
- ○ Not switching out on mismatches
- ○ Three going to trap
- ○ No communication or silence defense
- ○ Not communicating the screens
- ○ Not fighting the screens through or getting caught easily
- ○ Not helping in penetrations
- ○ Not recovering to their player
- ○ Not stopping the roll guy by tagging with a forearm
- ○ Not creating contact to rebound
- ○ Not pointing out a lost player where to go
- ○ Reactive defense or waiting for something to happen instead of dictating by being proactive

You should take advantage to exploit those weaknesses if you are playing against an opponent who gives you these 'signals' early on in the game. But, if, at first, the opponent team hasn't shown some 'signals,' you can take some calculated risk. Give the game some definition by taking extreme measures to assess how the opponent will react to different situations. This way, you are 'profiling' the team's 'personality' to use it to your advantage. For example, you can overload one side in offense, drop your players to the baseline, or take them higher. When you do this, you study their defensive weaknesses in making adjustments and testing their reading capabilities. You will then set a strategy to attack them by surprise later on during crucial moments of the game that you may see it's time to execute. Undefined defensive teams often chase their man everywhere. They break many of Einstein, Newton, and Maxwell's physics laws about time and space, motion, momentum, and energy, making your team inefficient and ineffective.

On your side, you must identify dysfunctional defensive or offensive system triggers and make suitable adjustments instantly before the opponent can read that on your team.

Do not wait for a long lead to make changes! For example, the flat players starting the game. I mean players being delayed on close-out or reacting late in defense to stop a dribble-drive. You know the player can play better defense at that point, but they start to relax and become overconfident.

So, early in the game, emphasize the sense of urgency by taking that complacency away. You can call a time-out or make a substitution. Why? The first five minutes set the pace. You don't want to wait until the quarter ends before calling a time-out or making a substitution, and you want to change the pace before any quarter ends. The worst thing you can have is having players closing out a quarter with heads down or arguing. One of the most extraordinary things is when they come excited, make the right plays, or come back even when we are down. But, many coaches' 'Ego Coaching' book says, don't call time-out early on; it makes you look dumb and inexperienced.

Let's get back to the point. This problem typically occurs at the beginning of the game or the beginning of the second half. Players need to be proactive at the start of the game. It is why the importance of the quality of the practices. We need to focus on drills that fix these dysfunctional problems.

Players need to see a board of do's and don'ts in the locker room. They need to know how the drills are intended to fix these issues and how the pieces go together to address them. Then, they can repeat it for themselves and work out at home to begin the new execution habits and translate them into the game.

When the players see the improvement, they learn how to trust the coach. They will trust the coach even if what is being taught doesn't make sense to them at that moment.

PRINCIPLE 20: COPING WITH LOSSES AND PREPARING FOR THE NEXT GAME

"We as coaches are responsible for indoctrinating the players in the right perspective in their sports endeavor. This perspective proposes a safe and prosperous experience throughout their journey and extends beyond the sports arena."

Here, the topic is not just about what we can do or think about winning or losing. Instead, it goes deeper. What affects players' character formation, skills development, and social interactions? What affects their capability to cope with winning and losing? As it is time and space-related and plays a significant role in basketball, the same principle applies to character and skills and their role in performance.

As a professional basketball player, I've seen many players experience frustrations, have unhealthy relationships with the sport, and make unhealthy decisions up to quitting. What was their primary reason? They were unable to cope with 'failure.' Failure here is not about just losing a game or not being able to accomplish what the coach, parent, and the players themselves expect.

The players, in reality, are losing the real 'cause' from playing the sport that goes beyond a game 'w' or a championship. As a player, my 'cause' was to go as far as I could in basketball to make myself and my family proud and enjoy any accomplishments, no matter how small or significant they could be. I wasn't obsessed or ambitious about college scholarships or degrees, making money, getting acknowledged (a little), or winning championships, MVPs, and gold medals. But, it happened eventually, as a consequence of focusing on smaller tasks and *executing the best diligent way possible*. Coaches are responsible for teaching the players the proper perspective in their sports endeavors. This view proposes a safe and prosperous experience throughout their journey, extending beyond the sports arena.

Coping Issue I: Lack of a Systematic Approach

"As a coach, we are not successfully considering the moral aspect's impact on their performance and development at an early stage; which greatly affects their game, motivation, and social interactions."

I have identified that players early during their formation are not taught in a systematic, logical, and progressive way. A player who can experience success and skills improvement can be more confident in what they do personally and how they play. The way a player experience skills mastery, goals met, and successes will impact their character formation significantly.

Like teachers at an educational institution, your coaching approach must be carefully employed and reflected upon to avoid setting up the players for failure. Coping with wins and losses will become second nature to all parties involved.

Here is a list of six 'coaching approaches' that causes players not to learn to cope with stressors related to wins or losses. These result in players having an unhealthy relationship with the sport:

○ Generic Instructions. Many coaches force the player to improve specific skills by yelling and repeating in a generic form, without preparing them systematically by progressions to support them in reaching the goal. For example, "You have to play hard" or "You have to play defense." These generic comments are not substantiated. It doesn't improve team or individual skills unless you have successfully prepared them physically and strategically to execute your requirements. Sometimes reminding them to make them conscious of the need for a reaction may happen. However, if you have not prepared them, how can you demand something they don't relate to? Regularly, these generic comments leave out of the scenario the 'How to.' This generic approach has some brutality from within, and it causes players to become guilty, skeptical, defensive, and defiant.

○ Unmeasured Exercises. Forcing the player to work harder, extra hours, extra days, or executing creative and fun drills is not the solution to improving the player's skills. Drills and exercises must be purposeful and have different parameters that enable the coach to measure improvement. Unfortunately, what regularly happens is that the players work hard and creatively without a target to reach. This takes away the objective of playing and the fun of the sport. The players cannot meet the coach's demands because it is generic and unmeasurable. The coach will never be satisfied with the players' performance. The players will also not be satisfied with their performance because there is no realistic target to reach.

○ <u>Winning Obsession</u>. Instead of developing players to face different adversities in a game, many coaches influence players to believe that the goal is to win. You can see that by their body language and actions. You can experience that after a team loss, the coach cannot cope with the loss either, and reflect that during practices and in preparation for important upcoming games. It seems more than winning is a personal matter rather than providing players the experience in the sport they deserve. In addition, players are misled by coaches using team generic comments to make them believe they are not good when they make a mistake or lose. Players will then punish themselves.

○ <u>Mixed Messages</u>. Coaches directly send a verbal message but indirectly send mixed messages with their gestures. For example, they say, "I am a defensive coach." But in reality, they go overboard celebrating a fantastic shot, not much as a great defensive play. They praise the best scorer player at the end of the game. The players will sense when the coach is prone to recognize and incentivize what is popular instead what others did to make the play successful. When the players lose the right perspective about the game, they suffer and feel they have disappointed the world, mom and dad. The players will try to cope with the situation alone. Unfortunately, parents fall for the same approach as the coach. To survive, some players will try to take the game into their hands, and then people call them 'selfish players.'

○ Changes and Instability. Teams/coaches begin changing players' positions, trading players, firing players, and striving to find the right formula to win games. They don't realize the mistakes they are making for their lack of knowledge in coaching the right way. Unfortunately, only a few coaches exhaust the resources in the players' formation before making organizational changes. In a professional setting, the team owners, media, fans, and sponsors play a significant role in influencing brutality in sports, making it unstable and physically and morally unsafe. These changes cause so many moral implications in the sports community that they affect the players' psyche. They lose perspective of the meaning of sport in their life, so many players and coaches become dependent on harmful substance consumption to cope with unfair stressors.

○ Marketing Coaching. Using creative and famous artifacts suggests they work hard, creatively, and intelligently. Unfortunately, this method is popularized fallacy; what makes it worse is that people believe it is the right way. Coaches promoting players on social media and dancing after a player's crossover are considered 'good coaches.'

I am sharing a list comparing the 'Winning Obsession Methods' employed by many coaches versus the 'Developing Approach.'

Winning Obsession versus Developing

'The comparison of the coaching and institutional thought process at most sports levels'

- ○ Obsessive Winning Approach Tendencies = find the best players from other teams => sell dreams and opportunities => offer constructive feedback to high performers => stigmatize the 'low' performer => long speech after losing => poorly offer fair playing opportunity = > force the 'lower' performer's withdrawal => bring new talent constantly => celebrate wins publicly and think they are doing things 'right' because of the winning result => needs to win badly again.

- ○ Developing Approach = cares about players' well-being => values their contribution = > fair opportunity to play and to demonstrate skills = > don't publicize the wrong => offer constructive criticism privately => retain personnel => are inclusive => celebrate smaller goals accomplished => motivate after win or loss => take the blame of loses but don't overemphasize it => do not fear to leave the team to protect player's dignity and maintain a healthy relationship => does not care to be called a loser.

Coping Issue II: Manipulative Stigmas

Players don't need unproven success from artifacts other than a ball and a basket to improve balance, strength, rhythm, coordination, skills, and the game. The problem we are seeing is that this marketing approach also seeks to popularize stigmas to their benefit. For example, great coaches may be stigmatized by negatively calling them 'old school' coaches. It suggests that what they know is 'expired.' 'Inducing' that the old school coach can't learn from the sport anymore.

This comments regularly affirms 'absolute terms,' 'hyperbolize' and uses 'out of context' responses to discredit others' ideas and introduce theirs as the truth. It is common in professional settings and e-coaches (i.e., online coaches). A new theory arises and impacts the market long enough to make a profit but rarely the idea sustain itself.

It is when another cycle of theories becomes the sensation in the market, mostly when the 'unconventional' becomes 'conventional.' Then you need a 'new' sensational idea (unconventional) or 'product' to impact the market. It is the same in other industries when science is wrongly used to their favor to take advantage by using the 'agnotology' approach.

The reality is that players are experiencing too many disappointments and retiring young. Their talents are not indeed developed and utilized, and they feel they did it wrong. Coaches must become more players' advocates, parent educators, and culture creators. They should restrain from using labeled words as they are used in a professional setting to manipulate behavior and get away with their ego intact.

Some coaches tend to label a player's action or comment in response to a coach's unrealistic demand as 'untrue' or 'unfair.' They quote captious words to hide their faults or lack of knowledge and make them feel guilty. For example, suppose a player is saying they felt pressured by a comment made by the coach. The coach will say, "You need to be resilient," inducing players to think they are weak. However, instead of the coach inquiring, reflecting, and identifying their faults and honesty, and seek to self-improve the approach with the player or team.

Another example is when the point guard tells the coach that the player got trapped by holding the ball more than usual because the player didn't have a clear passing lane where the player could pass to. After all, the the other players didn't do their receiving part of getting open on time. The coach will say, "Stop making excuses," or "Don't be disrespectful," instead of noticing the truth about the player's feedback and seeking help from the team to improve. Unfortunately, they manipulate the situation to get back at a player by indirectly ridiculing and put the player on the spot with their peers to humiliate and force revelion, having the perfect excuse to expell the student-athlete from the team, or even to get back at a parent. When a coach uses these manipulative words, we criticize the players for speaking up, making the team become dysfunctional and forcing players to withdraw from the group.

Coaches need to consider the moral aspect when teaching a skill that is not accurately measurable because their motivation and a sense of accomplishment play a significant role in the player's performance. It is not the right approach to throw the basketball at players so that they take shots in different areas by applying different moves. It is also not the right approach to have them make an almost unrealistic amount of shots from various spots. It is a fallacy the saying that this tactic indeed translates to the game.

The concept of teaching game situations is the right concept. However, the problem is using it out of 'context,' which is operated out of the 'developmental stage.' The right concepts are misplaced in conversations without letting the other part finish explaining the context to facilitate proper comprehension. Instead, coaches use 'cut-off' strategies out of context with truth. It is also a manipulative form of deviating attention (protecting ego) and inducing you are wrong. However, you haven't finished explaining the situation and probably never will get the opportunity to do it. It is common in any professional setting, affecting players' and personnel's emotional stability.

Coping Issue III: EGO at A Glance

There is another problem when it comes to coaches' egos. Many of them say they know if a player can play basketball or not because of the way they walk. Some say they can understand who can make the team without taking notes and assessing specific skills and the player's potential carefully. I do not understand this. There is so much arrogance from coaches overall; I'm not sure why. If we're going to impact the player's life positively, we need to reassess our approach to coaching. We should strive to improve continuously and accept that we need to learn.

Coping Issue IV: <u>No Plan of Action</u>

Coaches, before we go to an advanced practice section that enables the player to add diverse moves from different areas, we need to evaluate players more statically and progressively. We must deconstruct the skill to the level of its component. If we want to do this, we need a designed action plan. It is when the coach purposely begins evaluating the player using a self-made list of skills with a scale and begins making an assessment. The components to measure can be if the player uses the correct posture and mechanics in taking a shot from 10 feet. It compares the player's ability to adjust from when they worked the mechanic on the sideline. Then the coach models the correct posture and mechanics, lets the player demonstrate, and makes another assessment.

DESIGNING THE PLAN BACKWARDS

We must delineate the target to reach to help the team succeed by the training cycle required by the preseason, beginning of the season, mid-season, and postseason. Have an established end goal and show the team how everything should look by the end of the season. Then you list the skills that must be acceptable by each marked time frame. Once you have that design, plan your practices with objectives that meet those markers. Next, you must ask yourself: What skills should the players master?

Finally, you must ask yourself: What skills should the players master during the six weeks of pre-season? What type of offenses should they learn two weeks before the season begins? Then, during the season, you can go back to the plan and assess what has worked and what needs to be improved to meet that success plan you have designed. But coaches, if there is no documentation: How can you expect to identify trends of problems within the team and with individuals?

By identifying trends, you can have substantiated evidence to consult with players and parents and make a plan for private lessons outside of team practices. Then you will be helping parents to minimize expenditures on training sessions for their players and support the player to meet the required goal for the team's benefit.

The benefits of having the data are that the coach can decide to increase rigor and establish new parameters that may include a new set of skills. The player can see progress with the information, and coaches can identify and correct errors before taking the training to another stage. If not, we are making a player perpetuate a wrong posture or become more used to a form that may be detrimental to their game for years to come.

Starting with a static approach at their early training stage is helpful and essential to identifying the needs of the players, and the data will reveal the solution(s) to improve the team's problem-weakness overall. But coaches need a point of reference. Then, coaches can measure success while the player experiments with improvement and motivation, then add different spots to master in a game-like scenario. But, usually, players get frustrated because they do not experience success.

They hear generic comments such as 'play defense' or 'be a team player, and they are out hustling us.' This makes the team untrustworthy. The same situation occurs in any professional setting. In organizations, it is when the lack of trust starts with gossip, blaming, 'nobody knows,' sub-groups, and people being afraid to speak up and make recommendations in a brainstorming/team dynamic section.

Coping Proposal: <u>The Cause</u>

"We as coaches need to challenge what our previous coaches taught us and what we are shouting at our players will be backed up with a 'How to' and a 'Why.' Ask yourself, will it have a greater cause beyond the sports arena?"

When we strive to help players cope with complex scenarios, coaches have to reflect on what they, as leaders, influence and teach the players. Coaches and players need to have the proper perspective about playing or competing in the sport. We take away the 'cause' from the player if we only intend to win. It is like coaches are taking their dream away. Coaches must strive to teach student-athletes to become successful instead of winning games. There is a big difference; you can lose games and championships, yet you are successful. *Experiencing adversities and overcoming them develops a winning mentality from within. It produces a person with the confidence and conviction that no matter how difficult the situation is in life, you will overcome it through your proven experiences.* The following list contains seven significant components to teach the players the proper perspective by being more specific in our coaching approach:

○   <u>Specifics</u>. Detailed the effort observed, then praised it realistically.

- ○ <u>Individual Rewards</u>. Reward and praise the accomplishment of smaller individual goals. Help the players notice the 'why' again after being taught the 'how to.' They will be amazed when the 'why' is revealed after they have accomplished what you have demonstrated and explained. It is an intrinsic motivator that will positively mark their lives and those around them.

- ○ <u>Team Praise</u>. Reward and praise for accomplishing more minor team improvements and goals met. Give them smaller plans to meet by quarters or even half of the quarter in challenging game situations.

- ○ <u>Intangibles</u>. Help the team and model yourself to appreciate 'intangibles' such as good screens, dives, box-outs, extra passes, and opinions. The players will believe what they see and be locked into the team's 'cause.'

- ○ <u>Do not overestimate wins or losses</u>. One of my many amazing coaches once told me, 'Don't get too high when you win, and don't get too low when you lose.' We need to educate student-athletes to focus on the lesson learned about experiencing adversities (or defeats) and the opportunities that rely on it, instead of the urge to win and the disappointment to lose. Please note and remind them to go back in time and tell the players the lesson learned. What they have explicitly overcome by the adversity they confronted at that time, and ask them questions openly to let them reflect and share with the group.

- ○ <u>Essential Elements</u>. The winning of games comes from unifying the correct game-like elements, not generic words or plays from a dominant champion team. So, for example, you don't need to tell players 'to play as a team' or be a 'team player.' Instead, teach decision-making tactics (or cues) to trigger quick and safe execusions about when it is more appropriate to shoot, pass, screen, and drive-and-kick. When these elements are genuinely taught, the players will buy in, and teamwork will be revealed and reflected.

○ Concentration. During games, help the players focus on the team's strategies and formation, not on making or missing. It also benefits to avoid dividing attention by being aware of the surroundings. Major players' stressors (when they experience pressure and lose confidence) are when they are aware of the surroundings, such as parents and fans, the importance of the game, or the possession at hand. So often, you can hear, "Look who came to see you, and you need to have your best game." It is terrible. The player's concentration is divided by the messages coaches, and parents send, and the players will not 'buy in' on the 'cause' of what is happening in the game. Players may decide or execute what is not expected because of a lack of confidence due to the unnecessary stressor. Instead, *teach the players to focus on the right mechanic during the game and observe or reflect briefly on the other team's formation, strategy, or weaknesses. This mentality, redirecting their thinking to be conscious of the team's objective and a specific target, helps the player focus on the game and the long-term cause instead of the surroundings.*

As a leader, you can successfully influence the players to think about the proper perspective when you have the right mindset about the sport. You and the players will be able to cope with wins and losses. The players will give you the hustle, the movement, and the defense the team needs without yelling vague words. Helping the players cope with wins and losses plays a significant role in team success, but more importantly, it affects the relationship the player will have with the sport and the health choices they make.

PRINCIPLE 21: COACHES' LOCKER ROOM MYSTERIES

Many coaches will help other coaches with familiar things. However, they will usually not reveal the secrets of their success, at least not its most significant portion in the coaches' clinics. Also, we have to consider the time factor.

A successful coach likes to work on many things. These are hard to explain because they may not make sense to players, coaches, analysts, or media and may be considered weird. The best way to handle this is to keep it to themselves.

Do not restrain yourself from asking experienced coaches weird stuff about basketball. I know many of them will show you privately. Do not be afraid to ask. If you don't ask, then your source of knowledge will be what is in the media or widespread, and that's not a reliable source.

You should question what you see as popular. Yes, you need to put into perspective what is popular. Reflect if it is a common way of practicing from successful coaches behind closed doors. Social media promotes things that are not necessarily what good coaches teach. In an interview, the coach will only speak about what's generic and digestible for the audience to process.

You will never see a great coach wasting practice time. Every second is accounted for and valued. Successful coaches are masters at logically breaking down any play, drill, and situation to its component level. However, they are also highly demanding with themselves the same way. They pay close attention to small details and stress repetition, and take calculated risks in teaching something out of the ordinary. For example, great coaches will have players pass to the in-bounding safety man at the top on a press break at least eight times. Some 'basketball commentators' might argue that the game is not like that and that too many passes will force a shot clock violation. For that reason, inexperienced coaches discard this and lose a building discipline-habit moment.

Many coaches pass on an opportunity to build on the 'perfection concept.' They try to remediate the passing problem against the press defense by seeking out set plays all over the internet. They dare not take necessary risks and maybe lose some shot opportunities. They also do not tolerate criticism, because winning seems more meaningful so they can prove themselves. If there is no result, they blame the player's bad habits by appealing to the player's 'lack of IQ.' It happens almost everywhere, and it is an out-of-proportion mindset.

A Great Coach ...

Great coaches teach concepts that don't make sense to most, are not widespread, and are weird or extreme. Great coaches will realistically demand perfection, take players safely to their limit, and show radical love. Great coaches mysteriously measure success by the objectives accomplished, not by winning games, championships, or prestige. Then, it just so happens that they end up with a winning season. You will not see this coming out of their mouth publicly, and they will reserve it; it is why it stays a locker room mystery.

"What happens in the locker room..."

OFFENSIVE PRINCIPLES

"All the successful teams I've ever seen have three characteristics: They play unselfish, play together, and play hard."

(Larry Brown)

Indicator IV: Decision-Making and Awareness

Tactical Question: How can the players make effective decisions and minimize risks?

Principle 22: Offensive balance, threats, and matchups

Principle 23: Survey the court

Principle 24: Directing and leading

Principle 25: Spacing and timing

Principle 26: Movement reads and reaction

PRINCIPLE 22: OFFENSIVE BALANCE, THREATS, AND MATCHUPS

To help the players make effective decisions and minimize risks, coaches need to be aware of the skills required on the court. It is imperative to have a solid offensive balance, match them up to their correct positions and areas, and have the right combination of players on the floor to become a threat. Once this is taken care of, you increase the chances of making better and more effective decisions.

The offensive balance seeks to distribute players' skills and roles to maximize opportunities so that they do not conflict with the spacing on the court and create advantages for your team.

For example, if you have two good shooters, you may want them to go opposite each other. In this case, you seek an excellent offensive balance by strengthening both sides of the court. However, the coach also needs to be aware of the side you are putting them on and ask yourself this question: From which side can my shooters shoot better? Although, as you may know, shooters, slashers, and post players have a strong side, this is when players genuinely become a threat.

It will allow your team to have better spacing, as the defense will have to open up the court to match the players.

It will make it difficult to help defense by adding longer distances to recover and rotate.

Another example of good offensive balance can occur with the big players. If you have a suitable ball handler with good passing skills, you want your best screener post player to set a high screen on the ball handler. Then, have the screener roll if the player have a lower outside shooting percentage or pop out if the player can shoot from within the acceptable range. Once a passing or driving lane becomes available, the ball handler can increase the advantage by passing on time to the open player or attacking. The other post player can be opposite from the ball, positioning themselves to maximize the opportunity to grab the offensive rebound if the shot attempt results in missing.

If you have a great shooter coming up from a screen through the baseline and the low block, you want the shooter to come off the best screener. The coach decides on what side of the court will allocate them, considering their strengths and weaknesses.

A solid offensive balance seeks to have a threat in each of the positions or combine the fewer threats available in a way that puts the defensive matchups constantly at a disadvantage. Combining the player's skills you put together must align with your philosophy. You don't want the players trying to take the game into their hands. They must know what you expect from them.

Your offense will have threats performing on their strength and effectively in their assigned role and duties, by passing, re-bounding, shooting, breaking pressure off the pass and the dribble, setting good screens, or blocking shots. Because in a half-court situation, the best way to open the court or collapse the defense is to have a balanced offensive threat. For example, good shooters in the perimeter force the defense to open the court. A threat in the paint forces the defense to collapse to establish themselves into a position of advantage to double the post or help rebound. But, if the defense pressures your team at full court, you might have to change the alignment for better passers, receivers, and ball handlers to compensate for that. It will also increase the opportunity to obtain an advantage.

The coach will encounter matchups that might threaten your team and will constantly assess and re-align the tactic to turn it into a mismatch to their advantage. It can happen when the other coach surprises your team with a matchup working in their favor. For example, if the other team has a smaller lineup that is working and has the advantage, compensate by matching up with a similar lineup. However, when this type of situation occurs, you must prepare your team to take advantage of the size of your players before making changes without using your resources.

If you coach a group of inexperienced players, create progression drills during the practice sessions to sharpen their skills. From that point, assess the player's strengths and weaknesses in your practice plan, take notes and allocate them where they can be successful. Evaluating their strengths and weaknesses will help you combine them in the game and maintain a balance to have a competitive edge while focusing on development.

PRINCIPLE 23: SURVEY THE COURT

Why do players need to survey the court? Ball handlers must constantly see the open passing and driving lanes, their main 'escape valves,' the weak spots in the zone, and how the defense moves towards the ball from man to man. Players without the ball can cut or flash, but they must constantly assess the open passing and driving lanes. In that way, they can have the same mindset as the point guard and take advantage of the opportunity. That is when teamwork is at its best.

Point guards must ensure that their teammates are in position and ready to initiate motion to either screen, cut or flash to the open spaces. They need to see who is overplaying to trap, see what passing lanes are being denied so they won't compromise the pass, and see who is open instantly.

Some of the main questions you should ask your guards when starting a pre-season is: What do you look for when you dribble past half-court? What are you looking for when your teammate is inbounding the ball at full court? When a player dribbles passing half-court, they should be in an attack mode in a low stance surveying the court. It is a way to deceive the defense as they will think they are about to attack. The focus will be on the ball, generating opportunities for backdoors and skip passes for open layups or shots.

One of the main issues in basketball is that players are not studying the floor and expecting to break pressures by default. It is a problem that takes away the momentum to increase the advantage of the open passing lanes, the pace of the game, and the integrity of the space. Players should survey the court where their team is inbounding the ball at the other end before receiving it. When players receive the ball in a 'ready stance,' they should be prepared to push the ball by air with an outlet pass as the primary option but not limited to that only. Also, once the player receives the ball, they will look at the defender like they are about to attack in a 'triple threat' form. They will also do a smaller hesitation or fake to catch the guard off-balance and attack by land with their dribble.

Guards should know where to pass the ball is more likely to happen; if they experience difficulties, they will be able to find their 'main two outlets' at least. The coach will select at least two options as an escape valve whenever the team faces pressure difficulties.

Surveying helps identify escape routes and empty gaps for potential passing and driving lanes. Guards that know how to anticipate an opportunity will lead the players with the pass taking advantage of the open spaces. For example, they can bounce pass or make a no-look lob pass right at the spot to make the receiver sprint to catch it, or as they progress down the court, they can make a timely pass on the paint once a player ducks-in.

Players must initiate the move with contact to create sep-aration before receiving the ball from the inbounder. This improves the passing lane angle and gains more time and space to catch the ball and execute.

Players with vision are aware of their spacing. They will ensure to actively spread out on the court, setting screens away and cutting or flashing through the middle. Likewise, when players are inbounding the ball, they need to ensure that players are in a good position related to the proper spacing distribution and defense set or alignment.

Usually, against a pressure team, the opposite side's big man is open. Having that player flashing to the middle is an excellent option. As usual, the defense negotiates to leave the opposite last man alone. Another escape valve is the safety man relocating downwards by spreading out the court to open up a passing lane for the guard in trouble.

Guards must identify this, and coaches must teach the proper timing for this during different game scenarios. Guards need to know in advance their main two options when trying to break the pressure and before taking off by dribble. First, players must look at the same side to fake the pass and throw it opposite. The strong side is regularly being filled with defenders, and the last man on the weakside is playing defense between two offensive players. If the passer can identify this, you might have a 'double-tag' ready to catch and shoot as they have progressed passing half-court.

At youth level and in high school, they tend to dribble first without surveying the court and to be aware of the escape valve. The problem with this decision is that they are not giving a chance to the offense to allocate themselves into an area of opportunities. Guards disrupt against themselves the options to pass and effectively obtain an advantage by dribbling. So it is when players start entering into the 'trap.' The trap is the long lane by the sidelines where players regularly start dribbling from three-quarters of the court to the other end. I call this a trap because most of the time, the players will chase the tail of the ball handler through the sides like in football and trap once they pass half-court. The defense will force them to pick up the ball late with limited passing options, thus eliminating the passing lane and turning it over.

If players see an opening to dribble, they can do that with the will of stopping on time and making a pass as the defense is approaching. Alternatively, the ball handler can try to seek the middle constantly to widen the passing options. This way, your team will have the defense chasing late, risking the steal, and it can increase your advantage as they get left behind. Please remember that when players are getting pressured, their peripheral vision reduces. Hence, they need to anticipate this and constantly assess their escape valves. In addition, their teammates need to be proactive in moving into the passer's areas or angles of vision. Players need to understand how to move into the sight of the passer if we want them to make effective decisions and minimize risks. This can occur if the players who attack have the will to pass the ball on time.

Coaches can use a timer to acclimate players to handle pressure and improve decision-making by taking away the dribble as a rule in practice. It is a way to force players to constantly look to pass to the best option, to be proactive in screening away, and continually have them move into open spaces or opportunities. It is one of the many ways to help players relocate on time and anticipate threats or options when the ball handler is about to get double-teamed.

PRINCIPLE 24: DIRECTING AND LEADING

When guards survey the court and see some misalignments, they should be able to fix them immediately by directing and leading:

- before a teammate is inbounding,
- when they are inbounding, or
- after the ball is inbounded at the other end.

It depends on game variables such as the game's pace, the scoreboard, and defensive strategy. Before receiving the ball, the guards should organize its player to improve team spacing and identify open driving and passing opportunities. After a basket made by the opponent, if there is no fast break, they need to leave the ball down if they have to and immediately organize the players before inbounding the ball. Coaches must empower players with more basketball sense, help them lead the team from time to time, and give guidance when their judgement is affected by the heat of the game.

Players have to respect the leader and follow. Players must learn how to follow signal cues and the coaching board instruction. The Game Simulation section of the practice plan helps you make controlled live game simulations and use the coaching board to execute plays and tactics. It is helpful to use time-outs during practice sessions to give verbal instruction to the leader of each team and see how the team reacts to the leader's guidance.

Coaches will empower team leaders to make the call when there is no timeout left or when the situation is required. They must regularly get together on a dead ball and discuss anything beneficial for the team.

Leaders need to be communicative and proactive in directing the team. Not necessarily have to be the guard, and it will save much time and effort for the coach as they can focus on other things. Coaches need to have a champion's mindset, and every detail that increases efficiency must be considered thoroughly.

PRINCIPLE 25: SPACING AND TIMING

Some main rules on spacing and timing include one defender cannot guard two players simultaneously. A player cannot spread out too far from the ball when the opposite team presses and moves into their teammate's vision camp of reach to become an outlet. They need to move out of the defense's peripheral vision constantly. In addition, a pass must maintain or increase advantage, not reduce it. The passer and receiver must be synchronised consistently.

The concept of spacing must be aligned with the idea of timing, and they must be relative from one to another. For example, when going down to half-court, the 'escort's speed' (guards accompanying the ball handler) must be comparable to the ballhandler or point guard. The idea of timing is not just matching speed but also constantly repositioning into an area of great passing angle in the event of need and passing the ball on time. Your playmakers can't delay the pass to the receiver. The receiver can't be delayed or delay the passer, as the pass must maintain or create an advantage.

Formula: Constant Clear Passing Lane = (Minimum risk to steal the pass) + (Safe distance to receive) ≥ (maintain/increase advantage).

The concept of timing when attacking consists of two variables: while your player is making 'something' happen, 'something else' must develop. That 'something else' must develop to the extent that if 'something' doesn't work out, you will have another option ('something else') right on time.

Also, timing the shot is a must! Before taking a shot, your players must ensure that the offense is in their proper spots and aware of the ball and are not caught by surprise by the screening actions from big to guard or have their back turned. Suppose the player rushes a long shot and catches everyone by surprise. It gives the transitioning offense an advantage to go for a fast break as the ball regularly will make a longer bounce if the shot is missed.

It is why your team needs players with the skills necessary to create constant disadvantages by dribble or passes AND those with patience and notion of the timing. Patience is a must for the timing and can be drilled at practice using different game-like scenarios and a timer.

The 'stampede issue' is another problem caused by the lack of patience that affects the spacing and timing. It happens more at a youth level. Two or more guys rush to meet the ball to receive it from the ball handler. It invites defenders to double and triple teams as it is an advantage to the defense from the lack of spacing and timing. These forces the lazy lob passes, immobilize the dribbler, and take away driving and passing lanes.

Coaches must always emphasize passing on time during practice and games and ensure that the pass maintains the advantage or improves the advantage. Coaches can't have players constantly holding the ball for over two seconds. Players must trust their partners to make this principle possible. They trust their partner by anticipating the pass, leading the player to relocate for a better passing/receiving angle.

Even if the player makes a turnover by leading with a pass, demand that the receiver player needs to be alert and relocate right at the spot constantly.

When the ball comes to the side, and a player is two passes away, that player should be trying to get open. If the player waits until they are one pass away to get open, they might be late and kill the advantage. Players must understand that 'something else' must be developing while 'something' is happening to make the best use of spacing and timing. Coaches cannot have the players wait to do one thing after another.

The coach can use drills in practice, emphasizing spacing, passing on time and on target, and leading the teammates with the pass to defensive weak spots.

PRINCIPLE 26: MOVEMENT READS AND REACTION

You probably heard much about 'doing what the defense is giving you.' Most of the time, it is very accurate. Players must be able to modify their positioning based on the defense's spacing, their 'defensive triangle,' and their strengths and weaknesses. In that quest, the offense needs to make something happen. **They must create opportunities for others. It is possible in the following ways:**

- manipulating the defense's positioning by moving out of their far-peripheral vision,
- using different defensive cues as a signal triggering a reaction,
- setting direct and indirect screens,
- cutting deep, shallow cuts, or
- flashing through the free throw.

When the team moves constantly, it confuses the defense, disrupts their mobility, and opens many driving and passing lanes. Therefore, the coach must encourage the ball handler to continually survey the court to either relocate by dribbling and improving angles of passing to pass on time, dribble drive or take it to the basket.

Many players tend to relax on the weak side, waiting for something to happen. They must develop something. As a tactic, players can stay wide open to leave space for a great one-on-one creator, and you can use this when you have multiple skilled one-on-one players, and the spacing and timing principle is satisfied, then the inert state here may be the best option.

Here we have a problem. When those double-tag players are static watching the ball handler waiting at the wing almost to the corner, they stay too close, killing the concept of spacing and timing. So one defender can defend two players, and the other defensive player becomes a helper blocking visibility to the driving and passing lanes. However, this is just another game dimension that coaches can use as a team strategy. The problem with this is relying on one 'dimension.' The game becomes inefficient if it reoccurs.

Making the game inefficient kills the timing and opportunities for others who depend on a teammate to create them. The game becomes more stagnate when shots are missed or forced. It increases the difficulty to obtain the offensive rebound from your other players not being in a position of opportunities; it is a suitable additive to lower team morale.

Coaches need to remind players to do things that make sense to the team, not just for themselves. They need to identify off-the-ball cues helpful to making movement decisions. However, they must also identify signals that triggers an attack when they have the ball and are defended.

Here are some individual cues on-ball defense to teach players in benefit to the offense that triggers a reaction:

- If the defense has hands down – make an over-the-head pass and cut with force.
- If the defense has hands up – make a bounce pass with one or both hands, depending on the passing lane and the receiver's angle.

- ○ If the defense forces your player to their left – attack the left foot and lock it with your left hand.
- ○ If the defense forces your player to their right – attack the right foot and lock it with your right hand.
- ○ If the defense is flat – make a jab fake or hesitation attack and make a counter move.
- ○ If the defense gives you space – don't hesitate to shoot the jumper if you are within your range and have a good shooting percentage.

Here are some individual cues <u>off the ball defense</u> in benefit to the offense to react:

- ○ If the defense is overplaying you – go backdoor or screen away and seal.
- ○ In transition, if the defense is trying to match with a player – guard to guard will set a back pick at half-court to an upcoming teammate.
- ○ If the defense seems organized – the guard will set a back pick to big in transition at half-court to a static or upcoming big guy.
- ○ If the defense is guarding face to face – take them out far out from the play to create space for others.
- ○ For instance, if the defense looks at the ball – move out of sight. Instead, the defense tends to look back to where they last saw you. This time, the defense won't find you for a second.

Coaches will show the players in practice movement reads and reactions to help them improve decision-making to generate advantages for the team. Players need to value the little things that increase opportunities for their team.

DECISION TRIGGERS

Improve decision-making by putting rules into practice for the shot taker, controlling the number of passes, reversals, and skip passes. Controlling the game as a section in your practice plan helps you practice game-like situations meaningful to the games. It is also beneficial to teach them to follow instructions during time-outs.

Having 'controlled challenging segments' helps players practice decision-making and increase focus. There are many drills intended to develop focus, one of which is the triangle passing using two balls. It is a drill that requires attention; while passing the ball, the same passer needs to be ready to receive another ball and keep the timing and coordination of the exercise. This drill requires the player to make a good pass and, at the same time, stay ready to receive. This drill forces the players to concentrate and continue the drill, not just stopping and 'ease,' but having hands ready is a requirement.

Here is a list of tactics that will help the player in the decision-making process, which will enable them to see and react and brake pressures:

- If a player dribbles at you from the top of the key to the wing – you may shallow cut. Cuts can be in a semi-circle and replace the offensive player's last position. A shallow cut can be close to the free-throw line. The player can also flare away, get a handoff or go for the backdoor.
- If somebody is 'overplaying' – the offensive player can go backdoor, or the player gets out wide to take the defense away, as mentioned previously. If you do this, you are opening the court for your teammates. It is also a concept of spacing, and

you are generating an advantage for your teammates by becoming a facilitator.

○ If there is a gap in the middle – you can attack it to make the defense collapse. More likely, you have to be ready to jump-stop on time and make a kick-out to the open man or a bounce pass to the baseline cutter for a layup.

○ If the defense becomes reactive – you can make deeper cuts across the baseline.

○ If the defense denies the entry passes – players need to set a back screen or screen away before going to the ball. This will support the ball handler in having a more open passing lane before they are forced to make a lob pass by the aggressive defense.

○ Against a man-to-man defense – don't just go to the ball; players need to work their way to it. The player can reduce and increase speed to bump the defense and generate separation.

PERIPHERAL VIEW

Basketball is a game of cues, giving you constant information to help you generate ideas for executing the offense as it is in defense for your advantage. Some may call this 'reads.' This happens because there are some limitations, and among the limits, you can make the best use of the most efficient and effective variables. It includes and is not limited to the court dimensions, the number of players allowed to use in court, time and game rules, and the player's peripheral view limitation in a fast-paced game.

Based on this, Mother Nature gives you geometric figures, letters, numbers, and symbols to use to your convenience when creating plays, drills, and game strategies based on the game limitations.

Furthermore, it serves as a point of reference when teaching skills development and helping with decision-making, amongst other things.

With more variables you can control, you can increase efficiency. For example, you may find some weaknesses in the defense, such as poor third rotation and lack of communication. You decide to put a passing amount as an objective to ensure your players attack this opportunity and make the possession a little longer to identify a higher percentage shot opportunity. You can convert variables to your advantage as you can control them.

For that reason, you can begin to break defensive triangles in offense by moving out of the defense's far-peripheral view. For example, when the defense is focused on the ball in a defensive triangle, the player may have access to the far-peripheral view segment and see man and ball. However, the off-the-ball player can affect their camp of reach in vision by initiating motion out from sight.

In essence, the defensive player will divert the attention to the ball or their player, and the visual field is expanded beyond reach. It is opposed when the ball handler drives and kicks. The defensive player focuses on the ball, and the vision reaches close to a near-peripheral segment, thus increasing opportunities for mismatches for seconds.

If an offensive player moves out of sight (behind the player), they must modify the triangle. While this is happening, another player will also relocate on sight. It means relocating to the defender's camp of vision to force the player to modify the triangle again. In that way, you are not in your partner's area and creating indecision on the defense. The space left by these two players, the one relocating and the one cutting, will allow you to utilize the open spaces available. The best way to know the space to fill is based on the distribution of the players in the limited space provided, then do the same thing repeatedly.

Players will be breaking defensive triangles and are using the opportunity to create space for their teammates. Once the defense turns their face to look at the ball, your players have a small window of opportunity to call for the ball with an excellent passing lane, free up somebody with a screen away, or go for a backdoor.

Your player will create a series of events to your favor which includes; delayed closeouts, late switches, mismatches, open shots, and 2v1 layups opportunities. An important detail is when your players are flashing to the free-throw line 'nail.' If this happens, help your players identify possible 'spacing' conflicts, and one will relocate to find another area of opportunity.

Players who can identify potential conflicts in spacing are considered an excellent asset to the team. The coach must prepare your players to identify possible variances in spacing integritty and fix them instantly. In this case, relocating to another area or setting a screen away or a down zipper screen are safe options.

COACHING POINTS

You will see how the nature of basketball will give you options to execute more effectively and efficiently. It is how set plays are created, and this is how motion is born. You can control in specific situations the players who can cut or provide them with guidance. For example, only the passer cuts through the paint, flashes through the middle, or where you want the players to rotate if cutting away or ball side. Mother Nature will give you patterns to make plays and drills like geometric figures, symbols, numbers, colors, and letters such: as a line, segment, semi-circle, Z, C, L, 8, and so forth. You can use these to create tactics and teach points of reference in different sports when distance, height, width, force, and timing are involved.

Integrating the principle of time and spacing, movements, reads, and reactions into your everyday coaching plan will help you become effective in coaching.

Remember, as you can identify and control variables, you can execute better. You can even draw patterns from it and make them as set plays. You can also see how the pattern of motion is born; even though some may defer, nothing belongs to anybody. The movements, reads, and reactions effectively follow essential organic elements of nature and practical principles. You can control variables by putting some guiding principles and minimal exceptions representing a lower risk necessary for more remarkable results.

INDICATOR V: OFFENSIVE PROTECTION: THE COACH WILL ENSURE TO HAVE SOLID OFFENSIVE BALANCE AND SAFETY OUTLETS ADAPTABLE TO DIFFERENT GAME SITUATIONS

TACTICAL QUESTION: WHAT WILL THE COACH DO TO COUNTER-ATTACK DIFFICULT SITUATIONS AGAINST AN OPPONENT WITH MORE ADVANTAGES?

PRINCIPLE 27: Roles and responsibilities

PRINCIPLE 28: Safety valves and making the defense reactive

PRINCIPLE 29: Relocation and positioning

PRINCIPLE 30: Escort and protect the ball

PRINCIPLE 31: The passer and receiver's principles

PRINCIPLE 27: ROLES AND RESPONSIBILITIES

The coach will assign roles and let the players know the expectations of their respective position and the parameters of particular situations. It will maximize efficiency and minimize errors, which ensures an excellent offensive balance. It is necessary to delegate tasks based on the player's strengths. There are many tactics in each position that only the player who best fits the role can master, such as the point guard. The point guard should have good court vision, ball-handling, passing, organizational, and communication skills.

The point guard can perform many other tactics to increase efficiency, such as setting a guard to guard back pick in transition when they are off the ball in the weakside. They can also set a ball screen to create space, allowing the ball handler to split the defense and seek the middle causing a 4v3 situation. These are unique situations tactics to relieve the team from extreme ball pressure and the entry pass denial. It will force the defense to retreat and enable your team to run set plays or a motion offense more effectively.

The coach must set the standard and clarify who is a passer, a shooter, a ball reversal, who inbounds the ball, and teach in what situations to set screens. Hold players accountable for their tasks. Coaches are not to please players, parents, or coaches from the stance. Players have to earn the privilege to take shots or handle the ball to play freely. Build discipline first. The players need to master specific skills first; they can't just play the game without principles. It is the coach's job to find their capabilities and develop them. This way, they have more success and have fun. Nobody has fun when they get ridiculed on the court. They say, "Everyone deserves a chance to develop in other areas," or "Let them play freely." However, you can see the play is unstructured. While this is appealing and may seem true, we need to avoid putting the players in situations that may get ridiculed by the opponent.

Once the players meet the maturity level of their tasks, the coach will allow the players to have more freedom. This will help them develop their game in other areas and understand the different roles that are so important. For example, when the coach builds discipline and organization first, they will rest most of the game and redirect them. We often think we are acting in the player's best interest by giving them a free choice and positionless role. However, what is the coach's role? Think about a war momentarily: Do you let your squadron act freely? Or have they been trained to execute orders in specific areas they can master? Of course, individual warriors have the opportunity of judgement. Still, they prepare in the best way they can fight and succeed. We apply the same principle in basketball: don't just let players go out there without principles. It's not safe, and it may increase the chances of injuries.

SETTING PARAMETERS IN SPECIAL SITUATIONS

Most of the time, you will encounter that the offense rushes to the ball in the group when inbounding the ball, bringing the defense closer and helping the defense to have more coverage and control.

You will also consistently see one pass and a shot or catch and dribble, and collide with players. You see players going all-around at will with no direction.

It is essential to set rules in particular situations. In special situations, we provide strategies or tactics, mostly when they are regularly confused or ineffective in executing, to help players make immediate and most likely accurate decisions. For example, when the defense is pressing full court, the player who catches the ball in the middle in a return pass regularly looks at the player who passed the ball and returned it. Many times this reduces the advantage and results in a double-team.

The issue with this is that it gives an advantage to the defense because they can read it and act immediately to deny the passing lane and steal the ball. Instead, the passer can fake the pass and pass it opposite or return the pass once the player has faked opposite. But players have to get accustomed to using fakes; it doesn't cost anything, but very few players use it. The coach will review different scenarios or special situations with the players and provide the most effective way of executing them to help them in the decision-making process.

Another exceptional situation example is after an offensive board. The coach sets the norms of who can go up and shoot it or when to reset the possession. For instance, if somebody is behind the player when they get the offensive rebound, they must go up or pass it to the closest player to the basket. On the other hand, if nobody is behind because the player is in front of your player, they can give it back and reset the play or continue your offense. Especially in youth sports, players need time and spacing to take a good shot. You want to ensure that your team is maximizing opportunities.

Another example is teaching the players when to start the fast break if you want it after a steal or a long rebound. Be mindful that you don't want to play at up-tempo all the time because you will exhaust the players physically and mentally. Still, you want to take advantage of the opportunity to reduce falling into the traps and possibly take advantage of mismatches. By designating roles, you build discipline, hold them accountable, and help them succeed in a team setting. You can have the parameter to measure success and make from it to assess their progress better.

All the tasks assigned are part of the greater goal that the team has. So it is when you see teamwork take place. You will notice that players are not selfish. Most haven't been appropriately disciplined in their respective goals and haven't been taught unique situation tactics that create an advantage for the team. When there is too much "positionless" role, no structure or guidance, then you will see more "selfish players," most likely, they were just guided to that from the lack of sound principles.

By designating roles, you are creating to them like a cheat sheet for the less experienced players because players can't understand or read the game yet, or you can't just expect because they mature differently. You can't wait for maturation, and you don't have the time to ensure that. In practice, you will focus on small specific details, break down the tasks, and have them do as many repetitions as possible. After the repetitions, add a challenging segment to your practice plans, and you will see how much they improve. It will boost their confidence and give them a sense of organization, accountability, and skills improvements that genuinely translate into the game. They will look like a competent team and unselfish players, but it relies on how you as a coach empower them.

PRINCIPLE 28: SAFETY VALVES AND MAKING THE DEFENSE REACTIVE

When players are under much pressure, you will notice that they will get the ball and take a desperate shot. I call this a 'one pass and a shot' issue. They are not used to handling pressure or are not trained on what to do in different situations, so they rush the shot. Players should realize that they can enjoy the game more when they break half-court pressure, take better shots, and run plays.

An excellent way to break the pressure is using safety valve passes. Typically, a safety man player should stay back or at the top of the key. *These safety players have tri-factor roles and are regularly in sequence*: In a half-court situation, one of the safety function is to reverse the ball, start setting the play, and watch defensive balance if the ball is stolen.

The safety valve will be the player playing at the top of the triangle, the one in the back higher than any player. Usually, teams don't put pressure on this player. That top defender is used for a trapping opportunity in the sides, or the defense would defend higher-opening defensive coverage that weakens their spacing integrity. So, you can use this player as a safety valve.

Another escape valve is a big guy flashing middle if they are in man-to-man full-court pressure, we have to leave the middle open at first to let the ball handler or the one-man fast break attack middle. However, if the big man reads that, the guard is about to get trapped and confront problems, then the big man flashes middle.

The advantage to having the big flashing is that the defensive big can try to stay with their man, leaving the paint vulnerable. The guard from the weak side can go backdoor, expecting a diagonal skip pass. If the pass is successful, it can finish in a 2v1 situation. But, if the big man defender doesn't flash middle to cover the offensive big who is flashing, then you have an open escape valve in the middle. You might also have a more undersized guard trying to match that big in the middle. We know how deadly the successful pass in the middle can be and the confusion it creates on the defense. It is harmful because more than two defenders will have the impulse to try to jump at the big guy most of the time. But, this is an advantage you will want to consider as it opens many windows for the guards running through the sidelines.

Note: If the ball handler is excellent, everybody can go down to drag the defense with them and let them handle the ball from the whole court. Only the big guy escorts and sets blackjacks or sudden screens.

You can use a big in the middle in a zone full-court pressure to make the defense collapse and pass the opposite side for a backdoor. There are many variables, and you select the best for your team. But, to run a set play, you must first make the defense reactive or retreat by making timely passes. Dynamically, once they become reactive, you can start to run your play.

The guard needs to seek escape valves and demand them. It is why you dribble-attack to the gaps. To draw attention from the wing defenders and relieve your wings for an open pass, either coming high or exploding low to the corner. You will watch who is stagnating in reacting and redirect them. Stagnating players are waiting for the ball and watching their teammates get trapped. It kills the play's timing, giving the defense the advantage to overwhelm your players.

Remember, you want to eliminate any window of opportunity for the defense to obtain the advantage. You see this in the last possessions when their game is close in scores. The 'go-to-guy' has the ball, and everyone else watches.

- First is the most critical moment of the game. It is when you see the most inefficient plays or ineffective shots take place at any level.
- Second, players watching the play don't relocate or explode to the corners on time, creating a turnover for the passer as they are already compromised.
- Third, the defense is ready to help and will have a greater chance of stealing the ball or being in a good rebounding position.

The coach will ensure that the team is maximizing opportunities by breaking bad habits and will assign the role to the guard to hold the team accountable in these situations.

Safety valves can include the following:

- Have a top player on the triangle for a better passing lane, skip, or reversal.
- The big guy serves as a ball reversal at the top of the key. It forces the opposite big to come out. If not, you have a passing outlet which is a win-win situation.
- When there is pressure, the big guy is flashing the middle opposite from the ball.

- Strong side forward flashing or showing straight towards the ball as needed when there is pressure.
- Weakside wing to watch for the defensive balance relocating upwards to the top and fast when the guard dribbles one side in their opposite direction. The relocating guard will follow the back of the ball handler to become a scape valve.
- Best rebounder positioned opposite for an offensive rebound.
- Opposite corner man ready to receive when the guard attacks baseline (Normally, defenders close to the paint don't go out-of-bound to play defense, which increases the effectiveness of the almost out-of-bounds pass to the corner).
- Triangle rebounding whenever is possible. For example, both bigs close to the block and a small forward relative to the free throw create a triangle. It maximizes the offensive side's second chances, and the two other players can watch the defensive balance.

OUTLETS

To make the defense reactive and have them chasing, the players need to become an outlet before the passing lanes are denied. How can the players become an outlet? Players need to think one play ahead. This is possible by identifying triggers and assuming the pass will come so they can work their way to become an outlet and avoid pressures or getting trapped.

Triggers are situations in which moves or signals occur to help the passer or receiver understand their teammate will deceive a defender and become open. The coach is the one who teaches triggers or signs and safe options to make decisions that are helpful to guide the players to anticipate plays in different scenarios. Typically, coaches expect high IQ players to do this, they can, but there is no such thing; it is the coach who needs IQ and teaches this to the players in general.

The coach must constantly assess the players' adverse situations, annotate them, and create 'cues' similar to those on the 'Movements Read and Reactions' mentioned before. When the players assume that the pass will come, they will relocate into an area of opportunity creating a gap between your player and the defender. But, timely getting open requires a well-drilled team in different game-based scenarios.

Coaches need to break down at practice different game-like scenarios to show them the expectations when they encounter the situation and have them drill it until they master it. Here are some game-like methods that you can consider safe decision-triggers:

○ If your guard is over-dribbling, it will mean he/she is trying to attack the middle gap. The wing players know there will be a kick-out, and they will widen the court and be prepared to shoot or dribble drive again.

○ If the wing attacks baseline, the opposite wing relocates to the corner expecting the pass; also, the big guy expects a bounce pass in the paint.

○ If the wing drives towards the middle, the safety man at the top will relocate almost behind the attacker. However, the safety man will stay at the three-point arc and expect the reverse pass.

○ If the ball handler dribbles at the wing, the wing goes backdoor, and the opposite wing becomes a safety at the top of the key.

○ If there is a skip pass from wing to wing, the strong side corner says 'one-more' and expects the pass for an open three.

○   After a rebound, they need to know where their outlet person should be allocated and expect the ball with hands out as a target.

These triggers should be incorporated into the practice plan and repeated as many times as possible. These are game-like situations that will help the players in the decision-making process. Things like this are what make teams look cohesive and intelligent. Once the players master what you have implemented, keep adding some other scenarios.

To help the players master the 'art of anticipation,' they need to practice as many cues that trigger their decision-making process and rehearse them to become an action by instinct.

PRINCIPLE 29: RELOCATION AND POSITIONING

Players must learn the importance of relocation when they pass the ball, try to get open again, or even make a teammate get open. They need to understand the importance of relocation when they are one pass away from the ball. They must also know how to relocate when they are more than one pass away. The offensive player needs to have the opportunity of judgement to relocate and create for others.

Say the 02 player dribbles at the 03 player in a one-pass away situation. Then, 03 can go for a shallow cut, a backdoor, a flare, or a hand-off, as mentioned before. But, when they are more than a pass away, they can cut deep across to get a screen from the big guy on the opposite low block.

It avoids stagnation, and you will increase the chances for an easy layup or open shot. It is also great to drill in an early offense situation.

Relocation is a constant and combines the following elements:

- Aggressiveness
- Change of direction
- Spacing and timing

- ○ Weak spots utilization or outlets (escape valves)
- ○ Screens on the ball or off the ball
- ○ Slip in screens or reject the screens
- ○ Fake the hand-off (dribbler) or reject the hand-off (receiver)
- ○ Change of speed, contact, or positioning

When players are off the ball, players need to move into a relative peripheral view of a 45-degree angle or in the mid-peripheral view field of the ball handler to see their teammates. It corrects the problem of not having an outlet where to pass when the passing lanes are denied. But, the ball handler constantly needs to move into a position with better passing angles.

One of the principles of relocating is to do the opposite to the defense. If the defense is in a help position, the guarded player will move to a spot where the defense can't see clearly. The offensive player is breaking their defensive triangle. At least, they will confuse the defensive player by looking at the offensive player moving and guessing while the offense is attacking. They can't just let the defense read them.

Players' body language has to say one thing and their actions another. It is the 'art of deception.' It has to be a constant, meaning not waiting to do one thing after the other because they might be helping the defense to set up. It will help significantly make the defense reactive so your offense motion of set plays can occur.

Players must understand the art of deception on the court to successful position and relocate on the post or the perimeter. They must be aware of timing to avoid the problem of not moving, moving too slow, or too fast.

For instance, if the offensive player faces pressure, they can dribble back before driving to the trap, passing it forward, or changing direction. Changing direction before the defense forces your player to do so, and catching your player by surprise can be beneficial to avoid the trap. Likewise, if the ball handler is being chased in transition offense, they can change pace or speed to bump them and sprint again. It is the same when the player is off the ball and wants to get open.

Continually assess the defensive pressures and identify the weak link of the defense. The defense must give you something. In other words, any alteration from the defense to strengthen the strong side causes a disadvantage for them, and the coach has to find it and make adjustments.

PASS AND RELOCATE

When passing, the passer need to relocate by retroceding small steps with hands ready to receive it back with an athletic stance or meet the ball again for a handoff. Furthermore, it depends on the defense guarding. Still, if necessary, the passer must sprint to position backward and face the ball. Standing still is not a great option.

Coaches need to drill positioning and may use a timer for that. You need to put players in game-like situations to practice managing time and emotions when they are under pressure. If they don't practice game-based scenarios, you will see players get too anxious, and they will all stampede for the ball, killing the spacing and timing.

To reduce this issue, always prepare players for the worst. They have to expect full-court pressure when the opposite team scores. Players need to be in position as soon as the other team scores, and they will work their way in creating contact to receive the ball.

Then, they can interchange or cross by setting a screen with somebody to cause confusion and a slight spacing advantage.

Emphasize that when perimeter players are relocating to receive the ball, they need to make a small v-cut with their forearms ready to contact the defense. It serves to secure enough space to receive the ball and have their hand targeted outwards of the body to receive the ball.

Say the ball handler 01 moves close to their own player 02 by mistake when relocating. Then, player 02 can set the screen and pop out, flare out fast, or get a hand-off. But, the one-pass away offensive player cannot bring their defender to guard the ball handler without a tactic in mind.

When a player gets close to the other, bringing their defender can cause a trap or make the help side easy. But if it happens, you can teach them how to use the hand-off or commit even more to the ball going faster and set a good ball screen. Of course, if the defense decides to switch the screen, your ball handler will still have a small window of space to split. Alternatively, the screener will seal to take the defender out of the action momentarily, but this needs to be drilled.

Also, your ball handler can reject the screen by faking that they will take it and then going opposite. Leaving the screen also confuses the switching defense; all you need is space and time to create.

WEAK SPOTS

Players should use passing games by looking to run, stand or cut through the empty spaces. They need to stand in between players or confusion spots. Players should receive the ball outside the body or have a hand-out as a target. They should not expect direct passes when the area is packed with defensive players unless it will be a bounce pass.

Guards, when dribbling, need to attack the middle by a pass to the flashing big guy or guard, a drive-thru the middle, and kick-out to make the defense collapse and make them chase out. If the center is packed, then seek to attack from the wing. Especially against the zone, you can use reverse or butt screens that are great for splitting defenders when they force you to baseline or 'ICE' you. Players need to look for empty spaces while dribbling, and teammates know the relocation principles will flash out automatically to become a safety valve. They can use dribble attacks as a tactic after the 'passing game.'

Players who are trained and disciplined in this area learn to play like pros. They will look like they share the ball and look smart – all because they were disciplined in specific areas of great significance. Basketball is about discipline, not a question of IQ. Good execution gives the illusion that it was a drawn offensive play!

Players need to be drilled on how to survey the spaces before catching the ball, and then they will know once they receive the ball where their partners are. Players can't just focus on where the ball is; they need to use their peripheral vision. Players will then look at a point between the ball and where they would like to receive the pass. Receivers must become facilitators and unlock good passing lanes. They must move on time into a spot that the ball handler can see to anticipate the pass and reduce the risk of getting trapped.

Speed Changes and Fakes

Players need to practice changes of speed, indirect fakes (body movement fakes), and ball fakes. Speed changes are crucial to get the defense confused and guessing. Speed changes can be used when handling the ball or off the ball. Players can do a short hesitation when they are about to attack. When dribbling fast up the court, they can reduce speed and keep the dribble low after the transition to make contact with the player running behind to flip the ball to explode fast again. Also, when they are off the ball, they can dive into creating contact with the shoulder or forearm and explode out to receive.

Indirect fakes are moves without the ball. Players must dive and push off; they can do v-cuts and curls. Indirect fakes have similar objectives as ball fakes. These fakes freeze the defense, confuse and scramble them, and put the defender at a disadvantage. Here is a list of some fakes:

- Fake the bounce pass
- Passing fakes to the low post
- Fake lob pass
- Reversal fake
- Fake the skip pass
- Fake to return pass

Passing is deadly to zone and man-to-man defense. Make sure to include these elements when teaching passing and getting open. They must fake to create an advantage and get somebody available. The coach can use drills with the 'no dribble' or 'two dribbles' rule. It is excellent in teaching the fakes and making better on-time passes. Also, they can't set a ball screen. So, they must develop 'something else' while 'something' is happening. This great tool meets the principle of spacing and timing. It is a habit-building situation that teaches action and avoids stagnation.

PRINCIPLE 30: ESCORT AND PROTECT THE BALL

Players need to move with the ball when inbounding the ball at the opposite end after a basket. As it goes down the court, they should not leave the ball handler behind and turn their back to the ball handler. In addition, players must be alert because, with every move of the offensive player or every threat signal from the defense, the escorts need to react to become a helper.

Usually, the opposite player from the ball can become a safety valve relocating outwards towards the top for a better passing angle when the player at the top passes and cuts through.

Players need to drill speed concerning the ball. They need to learn how to run side by side with the ball handler. Then, of course, we must consider the defense's height, speed, strength, and ball handler's skills. The offensive guards can't go at a higher pace than the dribbler. They can go the same speed or slower when the ball handler is advancing the ball fast, and the opposite wing will slow down to stay as a safety.

One of the drills helpful to practice is the classic three-man weave. It helps the players get the concept of staying relatively within a sufficient distance and maintaining the pass's speed and spacing integrity. The three-man weave is helpful if appropriately implemented using the right objectives and emphasis. You can use it for diverse transitioning situations. Using the big guys, controlling dribble or passes, attacking the middle with one or two dribbles to jump-stop and release the ball. Also, to make a long outlet pass to score in less than 3 seconds, switch roles by attacking the sides. Then, add defense to close passing lanes to work on timing the pass relative to the defender's speed. It is a great conditioning drill that helps the skill of relocating immediately, intending to remain on the play and not just walk back once they pass the ball. Unfortunately, this drill is being criticized, almost 'banned' for new marketing purposes, similar to the suicide-drill boycott. Still, if this is practiced with the right teaching points and objectives, you will realize how helpful is.

The big guys' concept I mentioned in a three-man weave helps to discipline the non-dribbler players. They learn to be aware that they dribble when they have an opening because the guards are being denied. They can dribble but stop on-time from passing as the defense will chase to deflect the ball from the blind side of the big guy's hands. So create drills intended to have the player catch the ball on the move and stop, whether to go backdoor or reverse to safety. However, make tons of reps and emphasize the small details.

You must analyze the teaching points of the drills and have them on paper so you can review them and explain them in practice. If you have a big guy who you trust can handle the ball, let them have it, but ensure they have been practicing and mastering it. Awareness of the escort's principle will help you along the way when teaching. You will immediately identify and direct them when you see them doing the following:

- leaving the guard behind,
- not spacing enough,

- not seeing the ball,
- not becoming help,
- not sprinting into areas of opportunities, and
- not identifying cues against your team before getting trapped.

You can practice drills that include the player's speed, spacing, and timing. Work on full-court running 3v0 down the court, passing to each other, then adding one or two defenders between them, waiting while running down. Players will learn how to be ready to catch or meet the ball when the ball handler faces difficulties.

One of the advantages of properly escorting the ball is to correct the problem of deflections when bringing the ball down. The dribbler can't pass the ball to the guy running close to him/her a little faster as the defense approaches; most of the time is deflected. However, you can give it if they meet the ball, create contact, push off, explode to the ball, or liberate somebody with a screen.

While bringing the ball down, players can't leave the guard or have their back turned and not see the ball. Tell them they can't leave the guard behind unless there is a fast-break opportunity, but they can't hide when the guard is pressured or trapped. Assign the role to the guard to hold them accountable in this situation.

Players must escort and progress, matching the guard's speed. Wings who escort can't go straight to guard themselves by standing close to the defender at the three-point line. Instead, once at half-court, they must be able to gain the advantage over their defender. They should take the defender low as a fake to explode high to receive the ball close to the three-point line and avoid deflections. Coaches who send a big player in the middle against a proactive defense must assess if it is favorable whether having the big flashing middle coming from the sides by surprise or stand.

PRINCIPLE 31: THE PASSER AND RECEIVER'S PRINCIPLES

Passer's Principle

Ideally, coaches want to exhaust and force the defense to chase through constant passes until they drop their aggressive stance and become *a reactive defense*. However, coaches can accomplish that if players understand the relationship between passing and receiving. An excellent passer cannot make a successful pass if the receiver is not trying to get open correctly against a proactive defense and vice versa.

There are misconceptions about whom to blame regarding turnovers in passing, which happen in basketball, volleyball, football, and many other sports. With all the pressure the offense faces, the passer is often blamed for making a turnover or a delayed pass, which results in a decrease in advantage or lost possession. However, there must be a shared responsibility in a team, like a shared vision in an organization. Therefore, the receiver must be held accountable for the turnovers resulting in passing as long as the coach can thoroughly assess the situation and identify the source of the problem.

Receiver's Principle

A good receiver complements a good pass. The receiver can't just stand waiting for the ball; they must be able to improve their position concerning the offensive attacker. This will ensure a safer passing lane by improving passing angles. The receiver must use their best judgement on when to do v-cut, create contact, change direction and make fakes. In addition, a coach can use passing expectations or 'goals' during a game to help the coach analyze the other team. For example, they can use the *eight pass rules* to allow the coach to study the other team's defensive effort and rotations.

Internationally, it is almost a culture of playing by the air, as opposed to in the US, by dribbling. It also adds too many consecutive and fast screens. Mainly, they understand the passer and receiver's principles; as soon as they catch the ball, they already know where to pass (or, at least, you can see the intention to give). This passing game contains a lot of touches. It takes many repetitions and discipline to master this, but it does work and makes the game look amazing. It all begins with the harmonious synchronization of receiving and realizing.

I call the receiver's principles when they position themselves in a good passing lane and know how to anticipate pressure and sprint out to become safety outlets. They are constantly relocating in a ready stance to catch and pass the ball on time. They can increase the advantage through the constant passing game and getting teammates open with different screens before receiving. It is imperative to discuss, inquire, and study this principle as the game has different offensive dimensions, and passing-receiving is its core.

These are the *main three offensive phases* that interact from one to another in a cycle, helpful to diversify the game in the quest to find a better *shot opportunity*.

   I. Movement: Cutting, flashing, and relocating relative to the ball positioning.

  II. Passing-Receiving: Constant passing by releasing and receiving on time.

 III. Dribbling: Attacking the basket by 'land' or improving angles of opportunities constantly.

Any elements of variations added to this dimension and not limited to, such as screens, changes in speed, force, and fakes, are helping to make the offense effective and efficient.

Passing Game

Keeping the ball alive is very important, especially against a proactive defense. Players can't hold the ball and kill the advantage to the relocating player. They need to understand the importance of playing by the air, which relieves them tremendously from extended pressure. Players often hold the ball for too long when they feel threatened, over-dribble, or go for a desperate shot. Have them do a passing game to force the defense to be reactive, find gaps of opportunities, and keep the integrity of the spacing. They can combine with dribble drives, but illustrating them by actively passing is the way to find better chances at an early offense. Even if they get open, negotiate to say you want to trade a good shot for a better shot. In that quest, we are willing to risk and lose shooting opportunities.

Remember, some risks are necessary to obtain or work for a more significant objective. *If there is no calculated risk, It will be challenging to develop the discipline of teamwork; then, there is no measured growth.*

Players tend to do one pass and a shot because it makes sense for most; either they try to avoid a problematic situation or don't know what to do. However, try to teach them something that will make sense to the team's objective. When they go down to the basket with the ball, they act urgently to shoot or attack; thus colliding with somebody. Develop a practice plan that your main focus for several practices will be using a passing game. You can diversify by adding restrictions and small goals to reach, which is helpful to keep them engaged while working under pressure and building team discipline.

Opponents must have to find you as a pressure threat coach. If they lower the pace of their pressure defense and become reactive, you have a greater chance to execute better plays.

AREAS OF OPPORTUNITIES

The coach will stress drills to help the team identify weak spots or areas of opportunities and lead them with the pass to those areas. The passer needs to survey and anticipate the pass to the location. One helpful drill you can call a 'Weak-spot drill.' It serves to help to improve anticipation and lead with a pass to areas of opportunities, which can also be called areas of confusion.

You can use four offensive players to leave room for open spots so they can constantly receive touches in different areas. Once players get the ball, they can make a quick-release pass to an available site. You can add many variations, such as only passing to an open spot about to be filled. It will mean that the receiver has to move into an empty place for a lead pass. In this drill, have defenders aligned in different zone formations, and the offensive players constantly move into areas of opportunities. Then, the passers will make various passes called by the coach.

They must release instantly for at least less than a second. The coach can also time the release to measure growth and success. These are the passing elements that coaches can include in the drill:

- Over-the-head passes
- Chest passes
- One dribble and weak hand pass
- Bounce pass/Pocket pass
- Dribble-jump stop and pass

Coaches can modify the rules as they see progress and under-standing and ensure it is engaging and challenging. Also, players need to consider whether they can make a chest pass when passes are from a long distance. If it is in a short distance, then have them make a bounce pass. Once they accomplish the objective, they add difficulties using backdoors and ball screens and play live.

These elements add to the drill and force the offensive players to position themselves. Finally, the pass must increase the advantage by delaying the defense, having an open layup, or an uncontested shot. The different types of passes are necessary to apply to diverse game situations. During the drill, the defense will not move from their alignment, then add soft defense matchups as progression until the live game situation.

As a double-factor learning, you can tell your defense that they must arrive on time to make this more fun and challenging to the offense, meaning they arrive with the ball. You can consider an 'on time' closeout if the receiver receives the ball close to the chest or lower. It will help the defense to understand the expectations when closing out or matching up on time. However, it is considered a late closeout if the player already has the ball and is in the shooting, driving, or passing motion. Again, using different markers as a reference will help players learn various reads and react accordingly.

Typically, you can use this with the grade level of third grade up to twelve graders, and feel free to modify it based on your team's skill level needs. The double effect learning or benefit of this will help improve the deflection problem using the right passes in a given situation. Remember, players must be taught the 'target-out-hand' when trying to receive to avoid deflections.

In any drill, the coach must be aware that in the concept of spacing and timing, the passer will be responsible for increasing the advantage by delaying the defense in a closeout or creating a mismatch. Therefore, the coach will ensure that the next pass will increase the advantage. If the defense catches up late, the player can shoot or return the ball and improve their positioning again, but they cannot dribble to the defense to stop and pass. Therefore, the drive must be aggressive with the intention and capability to increase advantage and pass with time and space.

In trap situations during a game, you must look where those weak areas are left. It might have a mismatch opportunity that you may want to take, and the opposite side might be an excellent spot to start, making them chase by a skip pass. You don't want the ball in the corner unless you have a strategy. Just make them aware that a bounce pass is essential, especially when the passers are parallel and a defensive player is in the middle close to the passing lane. Because defensive players tend to reach for the ball, a bounce pass is deadly as they may 'gamble' to steal.

Building discipline is challenging because players and spectators tend to want a faster game, actions that lead to a quick shot, and their players' participation. Your teaching methods are unknown until all the pieces function harmoniously, but know people will question them first. Understand that, as long as you have a measurable plan, do what's best for the game, and you will earn respect. If you coach for others, you will never meet the team's objective, and too many people will be dissatisfied with your coaching capabilities.

If your team masters this principle and can execute faster and more efficiently, they will enjoy the game more, and team success will be much greater.

DOWNTIME

The safety guard should be a passing machine as the main threat. The safety person can be whoever is at the top of the triangle. As the player gets the ball, they already know where to pass it. But, the safety guard needs 'downtime' to survey the game and understand their outlets and potential safety valves or run down the clock.

Players on the court need downtime, meaning time to rest, study the opponent, get them tired, scramble, run down the clock, think clearly, and get relief from pressure. It is essential in any team; if players are exhausted, they cannot think clearly. As a result, their decision-making ability reduces and increases the turnover ratio, and their strength gets weaker too. However, what makes it worse is that they lose confidence. You can use any strategy as a downtime moment, but you may have seen coaches frequently using the 'Four Corners' tactic.

ATTACKING

Attacking the basket may frequently occur after the passing game. At this point, your team is creating delayed closeouts, and it is a moment to pun-fake and attack the gaps. The helper will close the driving lane. This is when the dishing to the big in the paint happens or when the kickouts occur.

However the situation may be, *make sure your team intends to attack the basket with the will to pass*. This concept is great for teaching players how to keep the options open when shooting/attacking. Coaches must emphasize this concept, which means that they are always ready to make the extra pass. Although, at youth level, you see that they struggle with additional passes. Once they commit to the basket, you know they are more certain to shoot it.

If coaches do many passing game-like drills and combine attacking to the basket, encourage them constantly to keep the ball alive using kick-outs and extra passes. It will create awareness of the attacker to anticipate the pass and see open looks. Your players will be relocating to empty spaces. They will always be under the expectation that the ball will come because they have practiced so. Coaches must ensure that players are passing to the open man. If they don't, it lowers team morale. Players will not see the benefit to keep relocating since they lose hope that the pass will come.

If you discipline your team in this area, you will experience the beauty of basketball. It increases team awareness and morale, and players will have more fun while expanding the opportunities to win.

Indicator VI: Understanding different offensive opportunities, defensive weaknesses, and attacking them constantly

Tactical Question: How can the Coach anticipate difficulties, use the element of surprise and prepare the team to succeed?

Principle 32: The opposite rule and deception tactic

Principle 33: Define the defense and get them scrambled

Principle 34: Breaking Pressures

Principle 35: Transition and fast break

Principle 36: Direct and indirect screens

Principle 37: Offense in general

PRINCIPLE 32: THE OPPOSITE RULE AND DECEPTION TACTIC

AGAINST ZONE

What is the 'Opposite rule' against a zone defense? The offensive players must seek to do what is contrary to what the defense gives. It means that players will constantly align themselves opposite the defense's alignment by using the empty spaces or weak spots left by the defensive team's space distribution. For example, if they are in a 2-3 zone, you can align them in a 3-2. These players use their weak spots to cause confusion or attack it.

For instance, if they play a 1-3-1 zone defense, you can align players in a 2-1-2 formation in a passing game. You can have names to different offensive alignments the same way you do for the defense. For example, against a 1-3-1 defensive zone alignment, you can use your two players close to the short corner way deep to break the defense's triangle. The player will be forced to decide whether to drop low or leave your player open. The intention to have the player aligned opposite from the defense is to move the defense to break the integrity of their formation; it creates advantages for your team. This way, you create a win-win situation, an advantage you want. Ensure your players are constantly moving, relocating, and getting ball touches before attacking the gaps.

From the youth to college level, coaches use a center player in the weak spots close to the nail by the free-throw line to confuse the defenders. Unfortunately, they don't realize why they do it, and guards force the pass in the middle, causing a turnover. Players must know that once the defense is collapsed, there is no need to push the pass to the middle as the objective is reached. Different shooting opportunities are open, waiting for your team players to take advantage of them.

On most occasions, guards take too much time in passing. They tend to hold the ball for too long, over-dribble, look directly at the player making the defense aware, or dribble at the defensive player killing the advantage and momentum. Coaches, make sure your guards are surveying the court and identifying this. Hold them accountable for not making a pass on time and unpredictably.

When players do the opposite, they must ensure they stand between two players. If a player stands between two players, the defenders will have to decide, and it might be too late whenever they choose to match up with the offensive player. You confuse them when they realize two guys are chasing one man. You can begin a chain of reactions if you stand between gaps until you get closer to the basket.

Generally, you want to manipulate the defense to collapse, especially the two closest players on the ball. The defense's typical reaction is to help steal the ball once a player receives it. It will create a mismatch or a disadvantage because two defenders went to reach for the ball. Players must have the individual ability to attack the gaps by dribble attack and ensure they are constantly using the gaps by giving touches to teammates.

Many times, you will see youth players attack without purpose. When they catch the ball, they make a bounce, almost automatically without realizing it. So we as coaches must emphasize these little things to reduce these 'mental mistakes.'

One way to teach the players passing and creating advantage is to have them repeatedly move the ball side to side or in and out unless you have an advantage in space and skills. Be mindful of letting the player decide without making aware of the expectations because they will believe they have the advantage and will not follow the coaches' direction. Instead, you guide them on specific situations to make sense of the team's general purpose, not just what makes sense to the player. If not, there will be anarchy and a power conflict in your group, something we need to avoid.

AGAINST MAN-TO-MAN

You can apply the same concept as you would do against zones to man-to-man. However, it requires more individual skills, focus, and effort. This tactic requires a great deal of awareness of spacing. If a player is guarding you high in a man-to-man, then go low. If they are chasing you and taking your space away, sprint in one direction, make a sudden stop and return. On the other hand, if they insist on staying too close to one of your players, just let the player know to take them out and spread the court, and you will generate space for others.

Say your guard 01 is attacking the left lane to the basket and have the advantage. Your big 05 is on the key opposite side from your 01 attacker. Then, make sure your big 05 will retreat just small steps in a semi-circle with hands ready towards the middle. Wing guard 03 will sprint fast to the corner on the ball side to increase the ball handler's spacing and be in their peripheral vision. Although guard 03 can flare away to the corner when the ball handler is attacking, it complicates the help capabilities of the defense. The corner helper on the strong side will have a longer distance to cover if they decide to help.

The weakside 02 wing who is opposite from the ball, will relocate fast moving upwards toward the top of the key, becoming the defensive balance protector. It will force the help defenders to make a critical decision in a short amount of time.

Another idea of the opposite rule is to attack the helper in defense. If the help defender is coming to trap, pass it to that man's person. You will have a counter-attack to the defense's initiative. Of course, you want to anticipate their initiative and attack it before the helper in the first rotation deflects the ball. If the ball handler has a quick release and has already made a successful pass, the defender, after a second attempt, will try to gamble and reach in to steal it, then the ball handler can fake the pass and have the first option receiver go backdoors.

To take advantage of the defender, the offensive player must be aware of their teammate's space. The receiver doesn't want to get in the ball handler's way when they are about to do something. So, something to do against the defense is to make the defender constantly find you and the ball. It breaks or modifies their defensive triangle, which is an advantage itself. Breaking their timing is one of the main opposite rules.

You want your players to stay out of the defender's peripheral vision, which affects the timing in different ways. It will delay them in helping or make them second-guess. So it will be a win-win situation. In a man-to-man, you also want to create long closeouts, which creates mismatches. It might be to your advantage, but one thing it makes is that one player will have to guard two offensive players attacking the rim.

There are exemptions to the rules that may affect it, but the basic principle is to do what's opposite – like when you fake one side and pass the other. As simple as it may seem, many coaches focus on playing by force, mainly forcing the dribble and the shot, but regularly, they do not reflect on it. For example, after a basket from the opposing team, they decide to press and trap. When your player receives the ball, they must always intend to pivot to turn forward, fake one side, and attack the other. It can buy an instant of time to pass or to attack.

Players must develop the art of deception. They must constantly fake, and their body language must tell a different story to have the defense guessing.

PRINCIPLE 33: DEFINE THE DEFENSE AND GET THEM SCRAMBLED

We don't want to play by force when playing basketball in a half-court situation. It is inefficient and a waste of resources if we haven't assessed the team first. Instead, seek to study the opponent using a passing game to see how the defense reacts, then attack the gaps. A disciplined team is willing to sacrifice a good shot opportunity for a better shot to define the defense. Then, when the players control the urgency to shoot or force the dribble attack, they study the defense's capabilities and deficiencies.

That is when they can manipulate the defense by getting them scrambled. When executing plays, shift the defense to one side to attack the opposite way.

There are many undisciplined defensive teams. Sometimes, it benefits them because they become unpredictable, and it confuses your players. Small good defensive possessions from the opponent might credit the defense and generate some sense of organization. On the other hand, they may earn false credibility from your players that they are doing the right thing and get discouraged. By defining the defense, you will make drastic changes in alignments to make an analysis and let the players see their most significant weaknesses. Once you identify this, you can set strategies to attack it, increasing team morale and leading to high-level performance. It is vital since the in-game assessment will help the coach select the best method to attack the opponent, instead of explaining something new at a time-out. At the youth level, you don't have enough time to explain and draw on the board.

To assess the defense, you will make drastic offensive moves to evaluate how they move, and then you can implement your strategy. For example, you can overload one side of the court, play high offense, give touches to the middle or low-post, and sag your players deep close to the baseline. A drastic shift in offense alignments and repeated touches (safely) will help you define the defense and know where to attack.

It's good to use open games to make drastic implementations on both ends (offense and defense). So you can use basketball as an art or science or both.

Of course, there are many variables to consider. But you have the right to take calculated measures and make adjustments. To make this work, you need to have the skills factor. You will need the players to be a threat (having a threat in each position would be ideal). If not, we compensate and rely more on roles. Although having at least two offensive threats on the perimeter and one in the post will help spread the court, you may depend on those threats mainly to increase offensive opportunities.

PRINCIPLE 34: BREAKING PRESSURES

SAFETY MAN

1. Have you experienced difficulties running your half-court offense when the opponent plays aggressive man-to-man defense?

2. Have you experienced frustration from your players because the plays are not working?

It often occurs because we poorly use a player for safety, and your players are unaware of the primary tactic they can apply to break most extended pressure. You can see online how many plays intend to break pressure. They have something in common. They all have this sequence: an inbound pass to a big or a guard when they (big or guard) flash for the ball from any area, and everybody runs expecting a long pass. The play may add to some beauty and may have players crossing or changing lanes.

Coaches must use a safety man in offense to overcome full-court and half-court pressure and force the defense to become reactive. The safety man usually is the man who inbounds the ball. Once the player inbounds the ball, this player can receive the ball back or a return pass for a potential ball reversal or quick tip-pass to the middle.

The defense usually uses the top player on the triangle to trap to the sides, leaving the inbounder open until the weak side help comes to a mid-point trying to intercept the ball. Then, it is an opportunity for an immediate pass to the safety and to reverse the ball, now that the defense has collapsed to help the strong side and leave the weak side open. But coaches, you are free to choose the following options:

First play option: Create a play to make a few passes and go. You may need to have more plays instead of variations (options).

Safety option: Have the player gain control over the defense and make them chase. You can add simple variations once they adjust.

The players need to execute this principle during the games consistently. Regularly, players tend to try to break the pressure by bouncing the ball repeatedly, dribbling down, and colliding with players. To make things worse, guards run straight to the three-point arc, leaving the ball handler alone, especially at youth level.

The defensive players often give your guards an open lane to the side to set a trap. Coaches need to illustrate this game situation during practice. Coaches will remind the player they can be led to the trap when they see an opening in the side lanes. Likewise, when players see a space to dribble down through the sides of the court in a straight line, it is a trap. They must control the urge to dribble down the ball, make them go aerial, or seek to attack the middle if they are dribbling.

Seeking the middle breaks the defensive press patterns as it confuses the defense and widens passing lanes for passing options. For example, the ball handler can dribble to the sides, change direction to the middle, and go across to the other side to return to the center again. But, again, it gets the defense scrambled.

PRESS-BREAK SEQUENCE

It is beneficial to practice some press-break sequence or process constantly, so it becomes the player's second nature when it is about identifying and breaking. It is crucial to decide who will inbound the ball, prepare your team for different game scenarios, and have ready different inbounders, but with *standard routines* and specific team language.

Disclaimer: The options you implement in any offense should lead to the original plan. It should create the conditions to return to what has been practiced once the main entry options are denied. If not, players will think they urgently need to break the plan as they already feel the plan is 'broken.' Because they rejected the entry pass, players sense the pressure and end up forcing and colliding with players, causing a possible turnover or a rushed shot. The 'standardized' alignment proposed here is just a safe template for youth. A higher level of basketball is easy and practical to implement. It will enable your players to execute with success by breaking pressure. If the extended pressure is not broken against a proactive defense, no set plays or team offense may occur down at half-court. You may have lost much practice time because you may have dedicated many hours running a set, but your team cannot execute it.

Coaches, you are not wrong by setting expectations on the positions and alignment you trained them for in the given situation. However, you are not making them 'robots.' You are caring for them, trying to help them not become frustrated by the lack of direction and being delegated a task that is out of their capabilities.

ALIGNMENT 'TEMPLATE'

The 01 point guard inbound the ball, then 02, 03, and 05 can stack up in a straight line by the free-throw line against a man-to-man defense or sideways against a zone press. The 04 player can start at the center of the half-court and move fast from side to side to ball side every time it is reversed. Once the inbounder signals hit the ball, the players open up to receive. You can add screen variations before receiving the ball.

Once your team receives the ball, you can use the following standardized elements to break half and full-court pressure against a trapping defense as follow:

FIRST OPTION

1. The 01 player inbound the ball to 02 to the strong side and steps in the court, and 02 will fake the pass ahead at half court 04 or middle, but pass back to safety 01 as soon the trap comes.

2. The inbounder 01 will reverse the ball opposite to 03 but can fake the middle. However, the inbounder can't pass and cut because there will be no safety (just for now). Too many deflections come by compromising the dribble, and the guard may lose control because they didn't have the chance to survey the court using primarily fake.

3. The middle 05 player can flash to the sides to receive as needed, but their main job is to stay big as an escape valve and progress up through the middle of the court little by little.

4. Wing 03 can pass to the middle or advance the ball to the relocating half-court player 04 to the ball side.

5. Player 04 will run sideways in the large center lane but not close to the sidelines on lanes A or B. I like to call the center

lane 'C' lane (C=Center lane) and the side lanes' ' A' and 'B' (A=Left lane or B=Right lane). Instead, the big 04 will go to the ball side, staying at the half-court, but can flash downwards to the hash marks relative to the 'coaching box' as an outlet.

6. Once the ball is advanced to either the middle player 05 or the flashing to the side player 04 at half-court, the opposite wing player 02 takes off. Wing 02 expects a pass from 05, 04, or the opposing guard in the weak side for a 2v1 situation against their safety 05 defensive players. Instead, the player will have a chance to get the ball close to the three-point line, ready to pass back to safety and begin the team's offense.

Here the sequence provides the correct elements of the distribution of timed flashes and touches necessary to break the defense's integrity.

SECOND OPTION

7. Say the wing 02 receiver in the ball side is denied or overplayed. Then, the inbounder player 01 can pass middle to 05 or advance the ball ahead to the relocating downwards player 04 to the ball side by the sidelines' hash mark area.

8. Suppose the inbounder player 01 safety is denied after the pass to the right to 02. In that case, the 02 receiver can pass it to the flashing weak side wing 03, cutting thru the middle diagonally as their defender will focused denying the safety. In this scenario, you use a middle big player 05 flashing to the ball side or put them higher to let the opposing wing 03 flash through the middle. If this happens, the 04 will sprint from the ball opposite as an exception, not to overload one side.

VARIATIONS

The coach can implement variations against zone or man-to-man defense after the inbounds, such as:

a) Guard to guard screens on ball reversal. The guard receiving the screen will be able to attack to the side since the screen will be unexpected. Therefore, timing the screen with the reversal is a must.

b) Big will set a back screen to the safety 01 after the inbound.

c) Big inbounds and stay back as safety and ball reversal.

d) Two guards open to the same side, and the second guard will receive the pass over the first guard and defender. For example, in most zone defenses, there can only be one or two players guarding a side of the court. Thus, if two offensive players open to the same side, it will create an advantage against one defender, destabilizing the opposite side if a second defender comes down to help. In this case, you're making a strategy that manipulates the defense to open a more significant gap.

e) Have one big at the other end to force the defense to have a safety defender and to move them to play diamond and one (1-2-1-1), a one-three-one (1-3-1), or a two-two-one (2-2-1). This way, you control variables and have your players practice these press-break principles until mastery. *At this point, you implement your strategy, not relying on only what the defense gives you only. You create the conditions you want for your team by provoking the defensive alignment that is more convenient for your team to attack.*

SHALLOW CUTS

If the opponent uses extended pressure at full and half-court, have the players do shallow cuts. Cuts should be shorter in a semi-circle, as mentioned before, to get the pass and make a quick attack safely. Shallow cuts can be when the ball handler dribbles at the wing. The wing will replace the ball handler's previous position by moving relative in front in a semi-circle form. The ball handler also can pass the wing, the wing dribbles out to the top, and the passer makes a banana cut in front of the ball handler and replaces the wing's last position. Another option can occur when guard 01 dribbles at wing 02, and wing 02 goes across the free-throw line extended to replace 03. The 03 players will relocate fast at the top as a safety. It can occur at full or half-court against man-to-man or zone. Of course, like most basket cut, the player cutting can stop on a weakspot during a shollow cut and have hands out as target to potentially receive a pass in the paint and elbow area to create confusion on the defense as the receiver can pivot turn to shoot (if half court), pass or fake and attack.

DEEP CUTS

If there is no pressure, you may have your players make deep long cuts. Long cuts force the defense to spread out and help the players know where the weak link on defense is. If the defense is passive or reactive, it is a moment to run your set plays and set the pace. If you are using a passing game, players who pass and cut can make deep cuts either on the opposite side or the same side after approaching the basket. Make sure they are in constant relocation with proper separation.

Players who cut through the paint should keep the defense busy by screening the big guy away to have the big flashing middle. They can also make a sudden stop and get an impulse from the defense with contact to get open for a shot, and the big guy can set them a screen to come out to shoot. It is an excellent way to diversify the game and make them get in foul trouble early in the game.

AGAINST DENIAL

When facing pressure, players need to liberate passing lanes constantly. Players need to relocate themselves for better passing angles and make contact with speed changes. The offensive players need to learn how to go for a backdoor. They must learn how to deceive the defensive players and work on the timing. The best additives against overplayed or denial defense to increase the chances of liberating passing or driving lanes are backdoors, backpicks, down screens, diagonal double-screens, and horizontal double-screens. But, again, this is combined with shallow cuts relative to the passer and indirect and unexpected weakside 'C' cuts on the weakspots.

COACHING POINTS

This press-brake process takes time and patience, not necessarily to be like that. But they can be applied against zone press and a man-to-man press defense.

Once players knows the press elements, they can break any unexpected pressure without calling for a set play. *As a teaching point and habit building, we must have the players practice as many passes and reversals as possible. Have them respect the longer process; if not, there will always be an excuse from the players not to move the ball and take shortcuts.*

Remember, to receive the ball in a man-on-man defense, players must cross from each other or bounce off a player to catch the ball. Players can't just go straight to the ball; it is often a deflection.

Also, in half-court defense, have them give touches inside and make constant fakes. It breaks pressures as it confuses the defense, making them shift to force the defense to become reactive by sagging. The benefit is that it causes the defense to get late on a closeout.

Remind the players not to go close to the in-bounder to receive the ball, at least not at first. They need room to see the defensive guards' alignment and maneuver to receive.

If there is a gap in the side lanes and they feel tempted to take it starting from three-quarters of the court, they can be misled into the trap. If this occurs, the player can dribble back and cross-over, seeking the middle.

If you have a great ball-handler and try to break the press, have the big inbound the ball, and everyone else goes back to draw the defense away. It is good to have the big to set flat ball screens, and it will be unlikely that the other big guy will trap the guard. It forces the defending big to come out; typically, they don't, which is a win-win situation. If the bigs come out, we have a better chance to attack the basket. Generally, the offensive big who stays alone with the guard at full court will be a safety. Ball reversal occurs side-by-side from the guard or in the middle as they get to the other half-court. The big can serve as a safety defense if your guard is trying to take it one-on-one from three-quarters of the court.

PRINCIPLE 35: TRANSITION AND FAST BREAK

TRANSITION

What is a transition offense? Transition to the offense can be a point in which the defensive players change from defense to offense. It can also be when the player steals the ball or gets a rebound in an active play. In this transition, defensive players are trying to find their matchups. They are scrambled because they are 'transitioning.' At this point in the transition, it is the moment for the offense to attack the defense's back as they are not in their best defensive position.

It is necessary to practice how to run the transition to maximize the offensive possessions for your team. In youth basketball, this is necessary as many teams 'sadly' play tons of zone defense and hinders players development, especially big guys. I no wonder why big guys-game is in EXTINCTION. Therefore, you don't let the defensive squad set up in zone defense. It will also be beneficial against pressing teams since you avoid them getting organized against your team.

How can we make the best use of transition? First, we have to take a look at the spacing we have. For example, when you attack the middle, your wing players will spread wide to run the side lanes. You will rarely see teams practicing defensive balance or transition defense. Usually, players get confused and are tempted to stop the ball at once by several players. For example, one of the generally accepted rules in defense is to stop the fast break in transition by saying, "Whoever is closer, stops the ball." But, if two players consider they are closer and go to stop the ball, they risk getting split, and you will have a 5v3 situation. It is an advantage you want for your team.

You can drill this with your team and make the wing players run wide. You might designate which lanes to run by each player and assign a number or letter to each lane (optional) as a point of reference. For example, your small forward can run in the weak side 'left lane A' as they have longer arms and can receive a long pass more effectively. If there is no chance to attack the middle, keep attacking the side but seek the middle as you pass half court. Coaches must emphasize having their players run out wide while escorting the ball while attacking middle-open options. When they see a potential trap to become an escape valve, the wings must be ready to return and relocate as safety men. Since you know that attacking the side can be setting your trap, you can attack the sides, ready to advance the ball ahead to 02 as a tactic. For example, if you have your player 02 running ahead of your player 01 in the right lane. Player 01 and can then pass ahead to player 02.

Ensure that your running wings are not running close to the side lane. Teams like to trap using the trapping pockets, which are the corner of the end of the half-court lanes. In this case, you need the best ball handler/passer attacking the sides.

FAST BREAK

What is a fast break? It is when a team attacks the back of the defense immediately as a tactic after a made basket from the opponent. A fast break is also when your team transitions to offense. Teams do that for numerous reasons, mainly to create a numbers advantage.

Many teams are lazy getting back to their zones or finding their matchups. It is why coaches use a fast ball-handler that can create and take advantage that the defense is not set. For example, in a fast break, you want to attack their backs and try to get a fast layup or shot. If there is no shot, you can run a secondary break which helps you take advantage of the scrambled defense as they might still be trying to find their matchups or zones.

Fast breaks intend to seek a quick shot to the basket when you have an offensive or numbers advantage. For example, if you have a 2v1 or a 3v2 situation, you want to convert fast by attacking the basket. In a higher level of competition, coaches have different norms for the break. For example, coaches might assign who runs the sidelines and who will cut deep when the ball handler dribbles at the wing player as they approach their offense side and are trailing through the middle. Regularly, the big players trail the middle as they are deeper in the defensive paint or tend to be slower.

Secondary Break

What is a secondary break? When the initial fast break doesn't result in a good shot opportunity, and there is no offensive advantage. Yet, the defense is trying to find their matchups. Players will immediately execute an early offense option offense opportunity without calling a 'set play.' Usually, a secondary break is an offense in which the players include more passing inside and use ball screens to create another quick shot opportunity. Its purpose is to make the defense reactive, stay unpredictable and difficult to scout, and possibly catch up with the score. When there is no rush in executing or no advantage, the defensive team is set, then the offensive may call a set play.

PRINCIPLE 36: DIRECT AND INDIRECT SCREENS

DIRECT SCREENS

A direct screen is an action that involves blocking the defensive player guarding the ball handler, and liberating the offensive player with the ball. On the ball screens, they are set without giving the defense a chance to slide over. It surprises them in their blind spot when you jump at the player for the screen instead of running in the player's peripheral view, making them aware of the screen. Screens require good timing from the ball handler and the screener on the ball. The screener should not try to force contact with the defender; make a small and long jump at the player, and their hands protecting their body.

You have to assess how they are helping on screens. Most commonly, if they are a switching team, you must show them how to screen appropriately when this situation occurs. Players get confused when they screen somebody, and the other team switches. When this happens, players need to set a screen to their own man, so the others come and meet the ball. The same concept applies when they are in a zone. In this type of defensive switch, either in man-to-man or zone, the defenders relay responsibility and wait for the man to come. The idea to set screens to own man is rare, thus making it very difficult to predict and counter-attack. It is also very helpful against inbound plays when they surprise you in the going zone.

INDIRECT SCREENS

Indirect screens are set away from the ball or the person without the ball. Off-the-ball screens or indirect screening are necessary. They are the number one in opening passing lanes and helpful in making passes on time. This leads to better execution because you want to create the advantage and have the defense run late on the offensive player. If they switch the indirect screens, the passer should pass the ball to the player that went to screen away because after they set a screen, they will turn and seal to get a pass or might slip and go for the layup. If they are not switching, then there is the opportunity to pass to the player who received the screen with the space or advantage created by the screener.

ATTACKING AFTER THE SCREEN

a) The back of the screener will show your guard the direction to attack. The guard will follow the screener and the opening behind their back. If the help defense, which regularly is the big guy, decides to play 'flat' to stop penetration, the guard attacks the flat helper. The guard then makes a pocket pass to the rolling big man who sets the screen.

b) Another option to attack the flat helper is to have the big 05 screening 01 rolling downwards, the guard 01 will reverse pass to the wing 02, and the wing 02 will pass it inside while the big guy seals and lays it in.

c) Let's look at a screen going towards the middle. If the defense decides to trap the screen or hedge hard on 01, the big 05 who sets the screen to 01 will roll diagonally toward the ball handler strong side low-block. Guard 01 will pass to wing 03 facing them, and wing 03 will pass it inside to 05 for a layup. (The offense 04 will pop out to the top whenever the 05 sets a high screen and rolls down)—cutting diagonal forces the weakside help-defense cover a longer distance, putting you in a win-win situation. Say players X4 and X2 decide to leave their area or man to stop the rolling big 05 opposite from them. Your 01 can reverse-dribble to pass it 04 ball reversal and 04 to corner 02 for an open shot.

d) If the defense forces your wing player to the baseline (people call it 'ICE'), you can have your big to set a quick 'butt screen,' the guard splits seeking middle, and the big rolls to the basket, positioning themselves for an offensive rebound.

e) In a big-to-big screen on the post with no switch, the guard will pass it to the coming center that received the screen. If there is a switch, the guard will pass it to the one who went opposite the screen and sealed the player.

f) If the bigs are in a stack screen on the block to release the coming shooters, if the wing passer sees the defensive big helping on the forthcoming shooter, the bigs will set a quick screen and slip. This slip-fake screen can happen in the perimeter when setting a flare screen or down zipper screen.

g) In the zone, if the bigs are in double-stack on the same post, the big who is higher on the block but shoulder to shoulder sets a screen for the downward strong forward. The strong forward curls to the middle of the paint to receive the ball for a short jump shot. The screener can seal and get the short lob pass to put it in at the basket. These are two options effective in zones and man-to-man.

AGAINST HELP-LINE DEFENSE

What is the helpline defense concept? It is a way of 'zoning' in man-to-man defense on the weak side to protect the paint from flashes or middle penetrations. Like any defense, it has its weaknesses, and the coach must prepare players to take advantage. The helpline defense can be the imaginary split line cutting through the middle of the court.

Against a team that likes to play zones, matchup zones, and help line or packline defense, the players in the weakside can set high pin screens or low pin screens to help the coming shooter. The spot-up shooter will also have more time and space to shoot. Against these defenses, attack it constantly with high, low, and big to big pin screens, and adding elements such as ball skips, reversals, fakes, and dribble attacks.

Especially, have somebody attacking the slots from the wing, skip the ball to the opposite wing, and pass it down to the short corner guy. Usually, this short corner player will be unguarded as their defender has to go out to help the helper caught on the pin screens. The weak side big guy can confront problems when rebounding against this defense. The big defender should be in a man-and-ball stance underneath or close to the basket. The defender can get pinned from the back with the other big guy after a shot and lose the rebound opportunity.

MISMATCHES AND VERBAL CUES

Good screening and ball movement and utilization of weak spots cause confusion and mismatches. What are mismatches? It is when defensive players are matched up against superior players by position or no defense at all. A mismatch is considered when the opponent has height, strength, skills, or speed dominance. It is something that coaches need to help the players to identify constantly. Players need to be aware of mismatches and exploit them wisely. Coaches can have cues whenever there is a mismatch. For example, call 'Open 5.' Their five players are playing against your best isolation smaller player on the perimeter. Alternatively, your best-post big man is against a smaller or weakest defensive player at the low post.

Signals or verbal cues are necessary, so it is important to speak one team language to become as less predictable as possible. Sometimes calling a name or using the 'fist' signal can be predictable but still challenging to guard and create an advantage. Coaches must be careful to try to break their offensive integrity to exploit a mismatch. Using the mismatch also must be calculated. If not, you may be driving away with what is working in your offense.

Sometimes, in a mismatched opportunity, the isolation player does not have to shoot it. Still, the best option may be to create an advantage. It means that when an isolation player takes on one and one, the defenses are static, typically waiting to close the paint. So it is when your shooters will be left open, and a kickout may be the best option. Teams often think that the player has to force the shot in isolation. It is also when you see ineffective shots being taken and good opportunities are wasted.

The coach must establish a team communication system to enable players to react to cues and verbal signals. It is a method that seeks to obtain an advantage proactively.

PRINCIPLE 37: OFFENSIVE IN GENERAL

Basketball coaches have an important task of constantly evaluating their opponents' set plays and continuous offenses. They need to identify the plays that pose a threat to their team and anticipate making adjustments to avoid them from running the play. Some coaches use set plays with only one option, while others prefer two or three choices in the set offense. Set plays are crucial, and it requires discipline from players to make them work. However, players must also use their judgement to take advantage of any opportunities that arise. For instance, when a shooting guard comes from a low-block screen, the screener may quickly 'slip' to call for the ball if their defender is focused on changing the route of the coming shooter.

Set plays can be a useful tool for your youth team. However, it's important to maintain the proper perspective when planning on using it. Your judgement can make the set plays work better in your favor instead of the motion offense and vice versa. Before running any set play, consider playing a 'passing game' or a motion offense to make the defense reactive. A passing game involves cutting through the paint, flashing to the free-throw line, receiving the ball on weak spots, ball reversals, and skips. Once your team has mastered the passing game, you can introduce set plays with much more effectiveness. Proactive defensive teams tend to disrupt offensive sets or patterns. This is why a passing game and motion offense with no predictable pattern per se will help inexperienced teams/players at an early stage and make the defense reactive.

Just try to keep the plays simple and seek fewer options in the offense because you won't have the time to go for a more extended play. The longer they play, the more ineffective it can be as it adds many more variables challenging to control. Here are some types of offenses:

- Motion offense
- Continuity offense
- Fast breaks
- Secondary break
- Quick hitters
- Set plays
- Isolations

One of the significant components of a set play is quick hitters, which is like a small version of a set play. It seeks a quick shot regularly when the shot clock is about to expire. Of course, this is not the only way, and some teams are just good at quick hitters because they have great catch-and-shoot shooters. Only you have to make sure to create some space for the shooter, and you create different situations by this. One of the advantages, for example, is that the shooters will draw attention and make the team second guess. This will leave your big man slipping open for a dunk, layup, or a corner guard going for a backdoor towards the basket.

DEFENSIVE PRINCIPLES

"Defense is all about helping. No one can guard a good dribbler; you have to walk kids through how to help and help the helper."

(Bob Knight)

TACTICAL QUESTION: WHAT WILL THE COACH DO TO PREVENT DELAYED CLOSEOUTS AND MISMATCHES?

PRINCIPLE 38: Efficiency awareness

PRINCIPLE 39: Leveling defense

PRINCIPLE 40: Generally accepted closeout

PRINCIPLE 41: Don't steal the pass, let them give it to you

PRINCIPLE 42: On-ball defense: Forcing and disrupting

PRINCIPLE 43: Off-ball defense: Triangular stance

PRINCIPLE 44: Limit the offense's resources: Energy, spacing, and timing

PRINCIPLE 38: EFFICIENCY AWARENESS

In basketball, coaches must teach proper body stance and a visual presentation of more efficient situations to contain the offense. This helps a team to gain an advantage and reduce the offense's effectiveness. Being efficient in defense means maximizing body movement to minimize waste and risks, and maximize mobility opportunities concerning time-space and energy. In addition, it will mean that while you increase efficiency, you reduce the opponent's effectiveness. When you compare and calculate the results, you have positive results that you can use to drive changes to your practice plans.

When you are efficient, you have a reasonable rate of contesting shots, decreasing shooting percentage and turnovers, and forcing the opponent into poor offensive execution. Being efficient also enables players to help on time and recover to your man safely and timely.

Players should avoid losing reaction time when trying to stop the ball on the strong side, and on the weak side help. How can this be possible? Players must be in alert-mode-defense even if they are more than one pass away from the ball.

They need to always be in the proper stance. They should control the urge to steal the ball when they challenge the opponent, and stop the ball when they compensate for their late reaction, lack of anticipation, and late arrival.

You want them to be proactive and ready for different scenarios. You want the defense to force the offensive player to turn the ball over to you by mistake, but you don't want to overplay. Here are some factors that delay the defender or put them at a disadvantage:

○ Hoping in closeouts
○ Reaching and hoping to steal the pass
○ Reaching in to steal on-ball defense
○ Trying to steal in transition or gambling
○ Not being in a man-and-ball position
○ Not be in an athletic stance
○ Giving a driving lane to the basket by widening the leg
○ Not having the conditioning for the game

Knowing what affects your team's defense helps you prepare practice plans to improve weak areas and build good defensive habits. For example, players frequently commit 'silly' fouls when they try to compensate for not being in a ready stance. It commonly occurs in transition to defense. Instead, when the attacker is already beating the player, the on-ball defensive player chases the ball late to deflect it, provoking a reaching foul from the side or behind the offensive player.

PRINCIPLE 39: LEVELING DEFENSE

You want to contain the offense and make it harder for them to get close to the basket. You also want the offense to drive to the trap or the help-defense and to lose the ball, utilizing fewer resources and minimize risks.

To make it happen, players need to drill to contain the urge to steal the ball, and they need to take space away and close as many passing lanes as possible. If you teach players the importance of reducing the offense's mobility, your players provoke the opponent to become more inefficient. This makes your team more effective. If that happens, you have an advantage. You win more terrain and use the shot clock in your favor. Once you gain terrain, the offense will react more desperate in making decisions with the shot clock against them. The offense may drive forcefully to the trap, make a late pass to a teammate without an open passing lane, or take desperate shots.

So when you have good defensive balance and the defense is set, your players can jump at the offense to trap from the blindside. Your players can get into position if the ball is already in the offense's hands. Your outside leg is ready to slide back to the side to absorb contact if the offensive player decides to attack.

How do we level the defense? If the offensive player initiates a motion, the defensive player does not go forward to stop. Instead, try to meet the player going back and up to a point to make them reduce speed, stop close to the crowded area, turn, pass, or get an offensive foul. The defensive player will try to meet the offensive player to absorb the contact. When that happens, the defensive player will put their hands out so the referee can see them.

Coaches, be aware that off-the-ball players must know when to 'fly' to the ball and closeout when the offensive player is about to pass. The ball needs to be released from the passer's hands. When the defense is 'flying' to take the space away from the receiver in a balanced defensive stance, the player will only make a light hand-check and quickly put their hands out. Once the player catches it and dribbles, the defense will actively force them to pick up the ball or turn to disrupt passing angles and force late relocation.

There are different footwork to use against a 1v1 defense. These are listed below:

○ The one leg up and another slightly back but to the side to close the possible driving lane. The player will have a protective leg to slide back on the move. The protective or back leg points to the sideline, the help defender, or an imaginary driving lane. The weakness is that they can attack the player to the up-leg, forcing them to open the gate. It will alter the defensive rotation and confuse the defensive team if they do not react on time and communicate effectively. The coach will review this game situation during practice sessions.

○ The other stance is flat-footed. The defender is not sending the offensive player to the help defense, just east-west. In a 1v1 situation, the player will have to hop backward when the offensive player is trying to attack.

This stance works better when the ball is 'flying on the air,' and the defense arrives with the ball. This way, the defense is taking space away from the offense by disrupting mobility, making it difficult to attack with momentum. The weakness of the flat-footer option is that the defensive player has less control if the arrival timing is not effective. They can get confused in switching stance once the offensive player hesitates to attack by taking advantage of the late arrival from the defender. Coaches can encourage players to contain the urge to steal the ball. It is safer if an offensive player hesitates with the ball, but the defense will not react immediately to steal the ball from anybody's fake. It reduces the risk of putting your defensive team at a disadvantage by letting the offense see an open driving lane.

There are weaknesses in both stances. First, you teach the best option for your team and consider the offense's strength. Lastly, being aware of ways to defend the ball in a 1v1 will help you create drills to prepare your team to minimize risks and increase efficiency.

It is essential to mention when a player in offense is moving slowly with a dibble, your defender can slide to stay within. Then, the defender can cross the leg and sprint to catch and contain when the ball handler increases speed. When sliding, it is safe to at least two times. After that, the defender can cross the leg to sprint once the ball handler increases speed. Be careful crossing the leg to defend too soon because the offensive player might hesitate or fake the move, and your player can get off balance and behind. Your helpers get compromised, creating a disadvantage for your team.

Principle 40: Generally Accepted Closeout

Practicing closeouts is imperative. It is one of the significant components in team defense that can help your team win a championship or lose it by putting the entire defense system at risk. A closeout is how a defensive player recovers from their defensive stance to approach the receiver on time and with a good posture. It seeks to avoid the possibility of a shot or dribble-drive penetration. It helps the player to be in good defensive balance and contain.

One of the best practices on closeout is when a player approaches a closeout, to chop their feet while still going forward, then to stop on time and with proper separation from the receiver. After a closeout, make soft contact with your knuckles on their waist and put your hands out (if the offensive player is not in shooting motion). You use that as a measure and stop their momentum but do not give the referee enough reason to blow the whistle. Or have a hand-out to block visibility and contest a possible shot from the offensive player. Then, when the offensive player puts the ball down, threatening to attack your player, they will have a hand-out and be ready to force the player to the trap. This takes away the offensive player's mobility options.

Many coaches stress contesting a shot using the opposite hand, which is the hand closer to the opponent's shooting hand. For example, if the shooter is left-handed, your player will have their right hand out for closeout and contest a shot. Another option employed by players is to block visibility to the basket by putting hands in front of the face. It helps disrupt the camp of reach visibility to the basket.

When a player is undisciplined in a closeout, they will tend to jump quickly to steal the ball or compensate for being late and reactive, making them vulnerable to a pun-fake and attack. Therefore, you can tell the player to jump and close out in a special situation. For example, a coach decides when you want a player to jump on a closeout. You may want to induce the offensive threat to fake and attack rather than shoot, especially when the offense is a deadly shooter and the defense is recovering late on the shooter.

In defense, when you hop to a closeout, you give the offensive player time to attack, get in a good stance to pass, or shoot, and you want to avoid that. Coaches can have players in practice working on sprinting out to the defender once the coach releases the ball and have the player make a quick hand check and hands out. The hand check can be the arm length safe distance parameter to play defense on the ball.

Against a quick-release jump shot shooter, you might want your player to cut the distance to a half-arm length to contest the jump shot better and induce the player to pass or dribble. Again, the coach will rehearse using volunteer players to use different ways to guard various situations based on an imaginary offensive player's strength.

PRINCIPLE 41: DON'T STEAL THE PASS, LET THEM GIVE IT TO YOU

When defensive players are one pass away from the ball and are denying the entry pass, you will see that players like to hop or reach out forward to steal the pass. It is a constant in youth leagues. They try to steal the ball instead of containing their player. They are also hopping in their spot with arms down and back straight. Therefore, coaches must remind players not to steal the ball, to contain the player, and force them to make erratic decisions.

In professional basketball, in transition to defense, you will see players trying to gamble to jump to steal the ball. It is often a lazy stunt not to run back on defense; they pretend to stop the ball. But this happens in youth's league because kids are undisciplined at this, and the urge to have the ball back betrays them.

We need to emphasize that and make drills to help them identify those situations and avoid creating a mismatch to the team and putting their teammates at a disadvantage.

However, making small hops is necessary in some situations to force a higher lob pass. This happens especially when a player is wide open and gets closer to the basket at the other end. It causes the pass to become higher and lengthy, maybe creating a deflection, giving a chance to the transitioning defense to set up or match up.

This situation can happen against a press but needs to be drilled. It occurs after X1 and X2 trap 02 in the side at three-quarters of the court and close to the extended free-throw line. The 02 who has the ball has stopped the dribble and is seeking a good passing lane. The X3, the interceptor in the middle coming from the opposite side, will make small hops between two guys, possibly to force a lob pass over the defense. It will at least make it complicated by reducing the passing lane's visibility of the ball handler to force a return pass to the safety player 01, who just inbounded the ball and might not be there as safety anymore. Some other coaches do that when pressing, and they use a versatile big guy to block the visibility of the opposite guard and contain the ball on one side.

These are part of special game situations that need to be drilled, assessed, and decided when to use or risk it. The impulse of players to steal the ball from the dribble, pass, or shot block is an issue defensive systems have been confronting, and coaches want to fix. So much is at stake. Coaches must discipline their players to contain the urge to get the ball back or get back at somebody. It is dangerous. Please never try to get back at somebody. It is an erratic decision since it leads to too many mistakes killing efficiency and effectiveness. Instead, show the players the importance of the following against the offense:

- o Containing
- o Disrupting space
- o Force the change of directions
- o Closing driving lanes
- o Close passing lanes

- ○ Affect passing angles
- ○ Block vision camp of reach

It is when your defense becomes efficient and effective. The turnover rate and shooting percentage of the offensive team will drop. Your defense will look fantastic, and it will be just by adjusting some 'misconceptions' about stealing the ball and changing possessions.

PRINCIPLE 42: ON-BALL DEFENSE: FORCING AND DISRUPTING

Once on on-ball defense, you decide where to force the offensive player. However, avoid middle penetrations or passes because they can cause communication issues. In addition, it's hard to define where the defensive help will come.

It can be drilled and implemented and be effective. It will require additional elements to reduce weakness such as closing or compacting the middle, pushing away the cutters and trapping the post more often, one pass away helper 02 or 03 to become more of a container or even switch more frequently with the on-ball defender. It is more complex and requires a higher level of mastery, but it can be great as well.

The challenge of taking extreme measures can be rewarding as it is when different philosophies are recognized. Even if some get the credit for something already created by many in the past, maybe get the credit for risking it, labeling it with a name, and making it succeed to the point of becoming famous.

However, teams majorly keep on the sides and trap when appropiate. Trapping on the sides gives your team the advantage of the sidelines. In addition, it reduces passing lanes to your benefit.

If the defensive player has to go more than two slides, they can cross the leg to sprint close to the opponent, trying to force them to change direction. Making the player change direction affects the way passing lanes are perceived, may cause them to lose the ball, delay the offense, and cause the player to pick up the ball, amongst others. Just remove the offensive player's space so the player can't gain momentum in attacking your defensive player.

Teach the most challenging situation or things that require more effort so they can easily dominate other vital things.

PRINCIPLE 43: OFF-BALL DEFENSE: TRIANGULAR STANCE

The body posture of the players must be in a triangular defensive stance when they are one or two passes off the ball or on the weak side. What does it mean to be in a triangular stance? It means to be in a position to help a teammate against dribble drives to stop penetration and recover.

The player in a triangular position should be sitting down, chest facing slightly forward, and arms wide open, maintaining visibility of man and ball. This stance helps a player keep their center of gravity and enables the player to increase their peripheral view instead of just sitting down and back straight up.

Suppose the off-the-ball-offensive player takes the player to the baseline by walking or sprinting out of the defense's peripheral vision to break their defensive triangle.

Your defensive player can try to make contact using their hands behind their back to get a feel of the player, and you can call this seeing with hands. Coaches must constantly drill defensive 'modification' when an offensive player moves out of the defense's peripheral view and is forced to relocate. Likewise, their teammates must modify their defensive coverage to compensate for the open-space to reduce weak spots, driving lanes, and offense visibility.

In a man-to-man situation, when they are one and two passes away from the ball, the players can sag at an acceptable and safe length on your command.

Players often tend to rest on weak side defense, and they do not realize the urgency of being in a good stance. As coaches, we need to emphasize the man and ball concept to have a player ready to react to their man and be in a position to help a delayed teammate with a stunt to the attacker and recover. The stunt to help in penetrations is like a fake by the player committing to stop the penetration and recover quickly. Often, the helper is guarding a good shooter, and they are a single-tag on the strong side that can't be left alone because there is no help. A stunt to the penetrator is the primary option to avoid the extra pass to the single-tag shooter.

Some drills can help with this, like 2v2 or 3v3 starting at the key. The idea is to have the offensive player dribble-drive. The helper who is at the wing can stunt, fake the trapping, or trap. The beaten defensive player can help their helper by switching in. If there is a mismatch, wait until the ball is two passes away to switch out. Also, they can trap the ball to make them pick up the ball and protect it, then switch out accordingly.

A triangular position and an athletic stance will also help you fight the screens. Make sure that the players are in a perfect defensive stance to help and recover, or deny the entry pass to the wing or the post. They should not just relax, expecting something to happen for them to react.

You can illustrate to them that an imaginary rubber band pulls them to a safe distance from each other and the basket. That way, they drop when they are off the ball in a solid defensive stance, and every time they go for a closeout, the rubber band pulls them again to be in a helping stance.

PRINCIPLE 44: LIMIT THE OFFENSE'S RESOURCES: ENERGY, SPACING AND TIMING

The main things in basketball that have the most impact remain the same and will never change: players need energy, endurance and strength, confidence, and time-space to execute successfully against a timer and space limitation.

Players need space to catch and survey the court, timing to receive to attack in rhythm, and time required to achieve when there is an opportunity or before the time is up. Therefore, coaches must focus their teaching tactics on limiting, reducing, or eliminating the opponent's resources, such as energy, space, and timing.

Players must be ready to play proactively every possession one hundred percent. The offense needs time and space to make plays and see their outlets. If the defense limits their space and timing and affects mobility, they also drain their energy and morale. When players do so, their peripheral vision is reduced near thirty degrees when they are pressured. Therefore, coaches ensure the players limit passing lanes that reduce the offense's space and court vision. Limiting space-time doesn't mean overplaying and reaching trying to steal.

One of the limitations in the offense for youth players is that they don't have the strength to make skip passes. They also don't have the patience to survey and release the ball on time and on target. As a result, you will limit their spacing and rush to make a play. Usually, role players will take most shots, something you want for your team's defense.

To make this possible, your players must have good conditioning. Therefore, having a conditioning section in your practice plan is essential. When you limit the offense's resources, you will disrupt their patterns and take them out of their comfort zone by being proactive. One of the major components of an effective defensive team is changing offensive players' routes when cutting from the perimeter through the paint seeking weak spots and better positioning.

Defensive perimeter players must constantly push them away or force them to the other help-defender to bump out the cutter to disrupt their space and commodity. For example, one of the best ways to protect your defensive system is assuming the shooter will cut after the pass. Therefore, the ball defender will not cut parallel or follow the cutter. Instead, the defender needs to create a contact or constantly get in the offense's way to find a weak spot to affect their mobility, but without affecting the defender's vision of the ball.

The off-ball defenders need to assume that the offense will miss the shot. After the shot, the players will bump away from the offensive player from the open routes to the basket, assuming they will crash the boards for an offensive rebound. This will enable them to improve positioning to box out better.

Coaches must proactively create a list of game situations where they can apply this principle. They should then have players practice, clearly understanding the expectations in those situations. For example, use video clips to show players how to disrupt the cutter's open lane, find a man to create contact, fake the trap, and disrupt offense mobility without turning a shoulder away from the ball.

TACTICAL QUESTION: WHAT RULES APPLY IN MOST SITUATIONS AGAINST A FAST AND AGGRESSIVE TEAM?

PRINCIPLE 45: Transitioning to defense

PRINCIPLE 46: Intercepting and disrupting

PRINCIPLE 47: Seeing with your hands and hips when rebounding

PRINCIPLE 48: Deny, front, deny, and make contact

PRINCIPLE 49: Constantly identify matchups and weaknesses

PRINCIPLE 45: TRANSITIONING TO DEFENSE

Basketball is chaotic. The defense has too many variables, priorities change constantly, and your players need to have the opportunity of judgement on what to do in most less harmful scenarios to the team. Therefore, it is essential to create special situations in your practice plan. Practice them in different potentially given scenarios, delineate some expectations and assign responsibilities to minimize variables against your team. You will increase the chance to control the offense as much as possible and facilitate the thought process for your players. You will align your players' judgement with the end goal.

It is also essential to consider your players' strengths and weaknesses. Avoid exposing them to situations that can negatively impact the heart of your defensive system and ridicule them.

One problem that can destabilize your defense is when a ball handler loses the ball and then sprints to chase the 'new' ball handler to deflect it from behind. Many times, it is just the urge to recover from a mistake. However, it turns out even worse because, on most occasions, the action will increase your team's disadvantage as the other team already has the momentum.

How do you solve this problem? One alternative is that the player can sprint back to find the moment to catch up and contain the ball handler. Another effective alternative to help a delayed player catch up is when a teammate stunts the opponent's ball handler, inducing the ball handler to reduce speed to allow your player to catch up and contain. Guards tend to chase the 'new' ball handler in transition right after losing the ball, or a teammate does it without considering the distance to catch up and the speed.

The given situation can have different variables. So, the coach can teach the players a safer expectation – not to chase the ball handler. Reaching from behind will often result in a late silly foul. In addition, it can compromise the next player in the rotation since the ball handler is increasing speed, and you team already has a distance and speed disadvantage. Regularly, it is the second person closest to the ball handler, with the ball at half-court, the one closing fast from the side to force the player to change direction to disrupt clear passing and driving lanes and use the lane to their advantage. Naturally, the player who loses the ball wants to reach-in to try to get it. Alternatively, some players will try to steal the ball simultaneously, putting your defensive system in danger.

Coaches should teach players how to handle this situation. Because your team loses the ball, they are at a disadvantage. You want to ensure your team is proactive in containing the urge to get the ball back but to recover from the disadvantage and not to increase it.

Suppose you have the ball lost and caused a situation that may compromise your big man. It is safer to have the trailer sprint back to protect the basket. The big man may stunt quickly to delay or force the ball handler to change directions to win time and facilitate a teammate to be of help. The trailer could then 'intercept' if a wingman is sprinting on the side towards the basket. There are moments when the player who lost the ball can chase the 'new' ball handler to get a deflection. However, that player must ensure a safety player is already running ahead to protect the paint.

In the transition to defense and after your team loses the ball, the last player closer to the opponent's half-court will sprint back closer to the basket. This player will watch the defensive balance by sprinting to the paint with an athletic stance and active hands, ready to contest a possible fast break, take charge, or close the ball in the perimeter. It can also discourage the player from attacking and may retreat. The player may swing it to the corner man. Once they receive the ball, the player in the paint can come out to help ONLY if no player is running to contest a shot and a second helper (opposite the ball) is running towards the paint to relieve the big man to contest a shot. Of course, they will contest the shot, but the paint shouldn't be left alone. Also, another player MUST be already matching up (converting) to the open man on the perimeter. In critical situations, coaches may need to compensate, and they may have to take risks and negotiate a lower percentage shot for a high percentage. It is why constantly practicing different transitioning scenarios will help your team reduce errors that result in a higher percentage of shots in favor of the opponent.

Suppose it is a guard who became the safety in the paint and not the 'trailer.' The big trailer sprints through the center to relieve the guard protecting the paint. Then, the closest guards to the strong side will match up in the perimeter. The opposite wing or safety guard will move to the weak side to find a matchup and be ready to be in a triangular defensive stance.

The offensive team is probably running their secondary break by this time, so this is when players can switch the screens to stay with their proper matchup. It is imperative to have some expectations to ensure the players are not scrambled and are oriented in this situation. You probably have experienced a good ball-handler dribbling coast to coast and taking an open layup. The players at any level just watch the opponent go for the layup. In most instances, some coaches don't drill transitioning to defense. The players mistakenly assume teammates will contain the player because they may be afraid to rotate. Or they might be blamed if they rotate and the offense scores. Or they stagnate, assuming it is the other's responsibility.

Coaches need to guide them and make them understand its importance and how it affects them. In this scenario, 'nobody belongs to anybody,' and they must do their best to help a teammate. But, they need to be drilling this with the urgency it deserves once they know how critical it is and understand the expectations.

PRINCIPLE 46: INTERCEPTING AND DISRUPTING

You will see many players that quit playing after an initial play. They execute one good thing like denying the entry pass in an inbound play, then that's it. Often when their offensive player gets the ball and passes by them, they will not rotate immediately. Instead, many players will jog back.

Instead, teach your players the following. If they get beaten starting from three-quarters of the court or at half-court, they must sprint back opposite or on the weak side up to a midpoint. There they can be ready to intercept the ball or to turn and stand in a triangular position. Intercepting here is not to steal the ball. It means intercepting the potential free passing lane. Say the defense is not contained and they are going into the fast break. Then, the intercepting player needs to go down opposite from the ball to be on the passing lane to potentially deflect safely the ball or last bounce pass to avoid the layup possibly.

If you don't drill this, most likely, you will have three players chasing the ball; the one who got beaten, the one-pass away helper, and a big guy who is drawn to play higher than usual. It usually ends in a 2v1 situation as the last weakside player will help the penetration, and their cornerman attacks the baseline to get a last dish pass for the layup.

In youth basketball, you may have expectations when a player is lost in defense. They can sprint back up to a mid-point to find the man closer to the ball that potentially will receive the extra pass. After that, the player will find their matchup and make the rotation necessary to recover their player to correct the mismatch or find their zone.

To avoid this, many coaches go immediately to the zone as it is 'safer' and simpler. However, we are not allowing players to grow, and we are not giving them rigorous tasks. So, they do not mature. As a result, we notice a significant deficiency in a man-to-man defense, and talented offensive players may not be selected for a high school, varsity, or college team. The reason? The defensive habit is not within the acceptable parameters to belong to a higher level of competition.

PRINCIPLE 47: SEEING WITH YOUR HANDS AND HIPS WHEN REBOUNDING

Youth-level players tend to look at the ball when a shot is taken. However, many of them don't react. It is almost as if the ball hypnotizes them. Players must continuously create contact against the closest man when a shot is taken. Big guys have a target on their back when their man is close to the block on the opposite side. Their movement is limited to following the rebound. Big guys must know how to protect their paint and 'push' away guards, to gain better positioning and space if a long bounce occurs after the shot. Getting good positioning depends mostly on assessing the offensive perimeters player.

When big defensive guys consider that the offense has a great shooting opportunity, they frequently identify whether there is a threat to approach for a rebound that may pin them. Once a shooting motion begins, most likely by the guard, the big guys should already have better floor coverage and a better angle. They create contact with one forearm, hips, or lean hard with the shoulder to 'impact' the offensive rebounder once the player has initiated motion.

Players need to know how to 'see' with their hands (before the shot to locate the player). It will help them to get a feel of where their player is so that they don't lose sight of the ball when a shot is taken. However, players cannot leave their hands on the offense because the offense will swipe the hand, and your player may lose balance, and the mission will fail.

As a defender, players must be at the helping point, somewhere between man and ball. Players have to have their butts down to use their body to lock the offensive rebounder when a shot is taken. Sometimes the player can't feel the offensive player going for the offensive rebound because there is much separation. Tell them not to turn their back to find a body with a forearm to create contact and box out. In that case, it is how a player can get off balance and lose the rebound opportunity. However, say the player finds a body and uses their forearm like a crabber. Then, the offensive player will use the defensive player's arm to push them down to get the impulse and obtain an advantage over the defender.

Instead, the player can still be in a defensive triangle and look with his peripheral vision for any player who is about to crash the board. The defensive player will use their hip to force away from the offensive rebounder and use forearms to get the impulse to their favor to jump to get the rebound. The idea is not to use the forearm to find and create contact. Instead, the approach is to initiate contact with the hip and then raise the forearms. It will be more effective when the player is close to the low block between the short corner and the basket and initiating motion to the basket. At this distance, the other helpful method is using hard shoulder impact if the player attacks hard with speed to the basket for an offensive rebound.

Say the box out is on the paint and the defensive player is close to the offensive player. Then, the defender can use their forearm and butt to make solid contact away from the pushing hands of the offensive player. The player can push out with their waist and arms wide open to prevent the offensive rebounder from escaping to the sides to rebound.

Players can find the closest man to box out when a player is close to the charge arc on the paint. The regular box-out here may be more appropriate since the player has no momentum and hasn't decided where to go for the offensive rebound. Still, it pressures you to box out to at least secure your area. A high rebound over your player may give the referee the impression of an over-the-back rebound and call a foul.

Essentials of Rebounding: Rebound is effort, tactic, and rhythm and also is required when to risk jumping to block a shot or not to stay in an advantageous rebounding positioning. The rhythm is reached when the player combines balance, speed, strength, and timing. Coaches, it is acceptable and safe to have at least three players making a defensive triangle to improve team rebounding capabilities. For example, one wing player may sprint fast close to the free-throw line, the other two big men inside the paint in between the basket and the mid-post. It creates a rebounding triangle to help with rebounding while two players are recovering maybe from helping and contesting a shot and becoming an outlet for a possible fastbreak.

Employing any contact as a form of 'box out' tactics depend on the scenario, distance, and speed, such as hip contact, shoulders impact, forearms protection, hand impulse, and butt separation. One major mistake in a professional setting is when two good rebounders are playing against each other. They encourage you to make a frontal face-to-face box out to neutralize the excellent rebounder and your player to allow others to get the rebound. However, it still creates a disadvantage for your team as the player you are forcing out can see the ball. If it comes towards the player, it can still flip to their teammates, even if locked by your player. In this situation, against great defenders, your smaller player has the solution. It means smaller defenders close to the paint will block or box out the best rebounder when approaching the basket. This is a great advantage because your best rebounder will be liberated. Also, referees tend to call fouls on big guys who are being boxed out by a smaller player and for pushing out "abruptly" the smaller player.

Players need to be obsessed with grabbing rebounds. Tell your big guys always to crash the board during practice. In the beginning, they will get exhausted, and their defensive capacity may drop. Still, after an estimate of eight practices or scrimmages, you will find that the ball will fall in the big's hands frequently. It will happen because they will have a 'rebound conditioning,' they will learn the tendency of the ball's direction by reading the shooter. Depending on the distance, players will understand the different contact tactics as an alternative to the 'old' box out. Players will also improve in catching the ball and keeping their center of gravity. Your team may increase the chance of outlet passes, which will constantly increase advantages.

PRINCIPLE 48: DENY, FRONT, DENY, AND MAKE CONTACT

Some scenarios dictate how to deny the entry pass at half-court. Denying the entry pass creates different advantages for your team but also has its threats. For example, if the player overplays, that player is at risk of a backdoor and affecting rotations. Also, your player may feel tempted to reach out to deflect or steal. However the case may be, it is essential to identify the best practices of denying the entry pass to minimize risks. The following list has four major components of denying according to the scenario:

○ The offensive player is static on the wing, and your player may approach the passing lane by extending his/her arm between the man and the ball. There is no need for contact in this situation, but your player is aware of the backdoor and has a leg ready to slide back. When a player is static at the wing and one pass away from the ball, the defensive player should be in a discrete passing lane denial and not lose sight of the player. Unfortunately, many players turn their back in a passing lane denial. They can't see when the ball is swung to the other side or passed to the deep cutter towards the basket. Poor passing lane denial results in backdoors and ineffective weakside help.

○ When the offensive player is at the top and pass and cut through the middle, dictate denial with contact, especially with the forearm, to force the player out of the ball's visibility or force the offense to disrupt spacing.

○ When a wing player is cutting through the paint from the wing, your defensive player denies passing lane and tries to force the cutter out of bounds just a maximum of two steps. The defender will turn to face the man with the ball but senses the player with their hands and body cutting through the paint. Once the offensive player comes out from the other side of the paint to the corner, your defender will turn and deny the passing lane once getting out of the block area. When the offensive player stands at the corner, your player can sag to a triangular stance. The defender has to be aggressive and anticipate the contact not letting the offensive player cut easily.

○ When the big is posting, block to block. In this situation, the defender must create contact and disrupt the route of the big man who is moving. For example, say the big man moves in front of the center defender. Your player forces the opponent higher out of their comfort zone. But if the offensive big man tries to move with force through your player, your defender will anticipate or react with strength and force the big to cut underneath the basket. Furthermore, if the big guy tries to seal your player, your defender must cut off the inner arms of the big man posting and stretch his inner leg out wide to gain balance and with butt down to contact hard the big guy and force again underneath the basket.

Note, if the big guy seals real aggressive, your player may let the player run over your player. The referee may call an offensive foul, or at least both are out of the play trying to stand again.

Always, you want your players to dictate by altering the routes by sending close to the help instead of letting the offensive player take advantage of the initial move or cut easily through weak spots (Open spaces). If there is no contact, the player who is cutting can seal your player. You want to avoid that situation as it can generate fouls in a shooting motion to the basket against your team.

As coaches, we need to teach our players to assume the worst-case scenarios as a safety measure. This will alert them and anticipate any potential move that can harm your defensive system.

In practice, it is essential to stress this deny-front-deny concept and 'Seeing with Hands' because many players get confused when playing defense. They make unnecessary rotations to guard the cutting player that they lose sight of the ball or their man. You can use some drills for this, starting from 1v1 to 3v3. You have them cut from the top of the key and the wings and ensure they are denying and making contact to force the player away from the ball. It is also good to practice at the low post. Have the offensive player trying to pass it from the wing to the post and a defensive post player denying three-quarters to the post. At the same time, the wing defender will be ready to create contact with the possible 'scissor' cut from the wing through the paint after the pass to the post to change their route.

Again, the wing defender can push away the cut closer to the help defense, or they can force the cut closer to their post to disrupt their spacing and free up one of your defenders to possibly help or short trap and recover, advantages you want to consider by applying the spacing and timing principle. The post defender can deny three-quarters when the ball arrives at the wing. The post defender can front when the ball is being passed to the corner, and once it is at the corner, the defender can deny from the bottom side of the post at the block by the baseline.

In most occasions, whenever there is an aggressive denial, your player denying may be at risk for a seal, backdoor cut, backpick, or butt screen, and you may want to have the help defense set and active, ready to help on time if there is a need.

PRINCIPLE 49: CONSTANTLY IDENTIFY MATCHUPS AND WEAKNESSES

To have a balanced defensive system, you must constantly assess the matchups. Assign your assistant coach to help you identify this and suggest substitutions to have a well-balanced defensive matchup. You need to be aware of many things, and a helping hand is necessary, especially scouting the opponent. For example, if you identify a player's weaknesses when dribbling, have someone pressure or set traps. If the matchup indicates it can hurt your defensive system, allocate the player somewhere that can be more successful. Find a player who can match effectively or with more dominance over the offensive player.

You must have terminologies that enable your players to react immediately. You must also have terminologies to switch players who can perform better against the offensive player in question with more dominance. On the other hand, if you identify that they also struggle with the passes, they lob it too much, jump to pass, or don't bounce passes, then take some risks and gamble to steal it. Likewise, if you put some ball pressure at the beginning of the game and experience dribble problems, plan on pressuring harder, setting traps, or going for a steal.

Being able to be in a perfect defensive stance will help you in your reaction, but also will help the player to read the situation and react if they are constantly assuming the <u>main five offensive actions</u> against your team: *a shot, dribble drive, pass, cut or screen* will come at any moment. This way, they can be ready to anticipate taking the appropriate safety measure. Your players will be concentrated or on 'call' when the situation is appropriate if they are in a good stance and assess the main five actions that can threaten their defensive system.

As a coach, you should love to learn about the players' strengths, weaknesses, and skills early in the game. But you also need to assess if they threaten specific players. Then matchup accordingly, or at least compensate by using great helpers-defender one pass away from the offensive threat to lower the impact of disadvantages.

You can make assessments early in the game prudently and safely. For example, you can have them play man-to-man, deny the entry pass, and see how they react. Then reflect on the following questions:

- Do they read and go for the back door?
- Is the team using constant screens?
- Are they using the big guy flashing in the middle?
- Can they leave the guard and open the court for 1v1?

You need to identify this by being proactive in constantly assessing their strengths and weaknesses to surprise them with different scenarios. For example, you can also deny the inbound's play.

Offensive players have a tendency to go straight to the ball instead of creating contact, and it is good to deflect or steal.

The coach is a student of the game, and you can't be too timid in trying different scenarios early in the game to evaluate the opponent. They will be the moment when you risk some possessions or even a few baskets. Remember, *there is no growth if you are not taking risks and learning from successes and mistakes.*

INDICATOR IX: PROACTIVE DEFENSE, SETTING TRAPS, AND ROTATIONS

TACTICAL QUESTION: HOW CAN THE COACH HAVE A PROACTIVE AND AGGRESSIVE DEFENSE AND PROTECT AGAINST AN ADVERSE SITUATION?

PRINCIPLE 50: Change of defensive looks

PRINCIPLE 51: Man-to-man traps

PRINCIPLE 52: Zone traps

PRINCIPLE 53: Rotating options

PRINCIPLE 54: Have designated safety defensive players

PRINCIPLE 55: Leveraging risks and gambling

PRINCIPLE 50: CHANGE OF DEFENSE LOOKS

A team with a proactive defense will force the offense to make a desperate pass, force the guard to change direction and over-dribble, and induce them to force shots to the basket. In addition, a proactive defense will play extended pressure. The extended pressure can be executed starting the sideline inbounds, at full court, three-quarters of the court, half-court, and even a strong entry pass denial.

They seek to make sudden changes in defensive tactics or 'change of looks.' For example, the defense will fake the full-court pressure to evaluate weak points, fake the traps, shift from man-to-man to zone, and vice-versa.

A proactive defense will put extreme ball pressure making the ball-handling very difficult, reducing driving and passing lanes. Additionally, a proactive team seeks to establish the game's tempo instead of letting the offense dictate. Teams that wait for an offensive set play to occur are usually reactive.

A reactive defense lets teams come from full-court with no pressure, or are not denying the inbound entry pass, and are playing low defense at half-court. The advantage of this defense is that it protects your players from exhaustion and reduces the risks of injuries. The disadvantage is that the offense will have your players guessing what will happen next. The coach can use this defensive tactic if they are confident in the team's communication skills. As coaches, we must reduce variables that put our players to guess. Instead, we want to dictate by changing defensive looks, which may decrease the threat of your defensive system against a well-prepared team.

PRINCIPLE 51: MAN-TO-MAN TRAPS

GENERALLY ACCEPTED TRAPS

Usually, when setting traps, there will be two players trapping, and two can become the interceptors. The last man can be the safety man. You can establish that the safety man is the last person in the rotation, typically the person on the opposite side and splitting two players at the bottom. Although there must always be a person playing between two (splitting) when you trap, ensure it is the last person because the skip pass is difficult to make. Many coaches negotiate this by leaving the last opposite man open.

In a man-to-man defense, while pressuring the ball, we seek to force a turnover, a lob pass, direction changes to close passing and driving lanes, or a violation on the shot clock. However, we need to seek to trap if it is needed.

How can we trap in man-to-man? By going to the blindside for most. For example, in half-court defense, say your X1 is defending 01. When 01 passes the ball to the 02 wing, X1 will follow to trap from the side or almost from behind the player. They call it 'the blind side.' We need to ensure that the other player close to the middle of the nail is playing ball denial close to the big guy, we don't want the ball in the middle, and if it happens, we drop the pressure and find the match-up again. Coaches need to ensure that in this situation, the opposite X3 wing will rotate up fast to deny or risk to intercept the pass back to 01, who is at the top and decided to stay as 'safety' and didn't cut.

Another way to trap in man-to-man is when the guard 01 is a threat, and we want to force them to release the ball as early as possible. An excellent way to trap is if the 05 trailer is close to the guard 01 and the guard has inadequate spacing. Then, your X5 will trap hard for a second or two to 01 and return to 05. Then, if the big 05 decides to roll to the basket, the closest defender wing player sags to tag the big with a forearm for a second or two while X5 recovers back. Again, we want to force their 05 to start the play at the top and not the ball handler most of the time. It is also good against a secondary break. For example, if the big 05 goes for the pick and roll, you can have your big X5 anticipate and trap very high. It will lead the passing guard to release the ball fast to the big rolling guy outside the paint, an advantage you want in putting their big in a problematic situation.

You may want to take advantage from this scenario because the rolling big will be so far out that the help will be waiting, and the big will either try to force a shot or a pass, a risk that you want to live with. Worst case scenario, the big pops out as safety to reverse the ball. It will give your big player a chance to convert or find their matchup leaving the opposite team a few seconds on the shot clock.

Another scenario is using the wings X2 or X3 to jump-trap high to the ball handler 01 by the surprise element, and the coach will set norms from which side the help trap will come. Typically, from the side, you will have a player playing close to the corner that can rotate up as in a 4-out and one-in to cover the wing. The wing offensive player might get the lob pass if the ball handler releases the ball quickly because of the pressure trap. Ideally, in this scenario it can be the X4 that will shift higher to intercept. But the wings need to be in ball denial or almost overplaying to enable them to shorten the distance to go to trap once the 01 passes half-court.

The same principle applies to trapping the post. Of course, you can use the opposite player in the paint (whoever is closer to the opposite block) to trap from the blindside, which is from the baseline, but it can vary. The trap can come from different areas, such as the same side wing and opposite wing close to the opposite elbow. However, ensure that the trapper is coming from the weakest link of the offense to reduce risks.

The coach's responsibility is to practice different trap scenarios and adequately allocate the key players to maximize the opportunity to steal the ball back or force a turnover. By practicing the traps, the coach will identify key players that are good for trapping and designate them as trappers, meaning they can jump to the trap by surprise in a given scenario.

You can set other traps in a man-to-man, for example, only trapping whenever the ball is passed to the corner. Make sure that the next player is in a triangular defensive stance and ready to jump fast to the open defender.

Say nothing happens after the initial trap, and you decide to have them drawback to find the matchup. Then, the player that was trapping that created a mismatch must sprint and find their player and switch out. They can do it when they are two passes away. Demand they must arrive on time and ensure it is safe.

PRINCIPLE 52: ZONE TRAPS

FLYING TRAPS

There are many ways to set traps in a zone, but it is common to use zone traps from the triangle areas of that zone formation. For example, the 1-2-2, 1-3-1, 3-2, and 1-2-1-1. These zones give you three players at the top, which can form a triangle. Once the top player and the strong side wing trap, the opposite wing relocates higher to a midpoint to form the triangle. By the moment the ball handler is given a side towards the wing, it is indicative that the first two guys in the zone closer to the ball handler will be trapping. Alternatively, if X1 at the top forces the 01 to pass the side to 02. As soon as it happens, X1 can sprint immediately to trap 02. The opposite wing X3 moves up to protect the top zone by intercepting the open lane to the basket and in front of the top of the key player. It is similar to man-to-man. It is the most common and simple way to set traps. Coaches must drill this and prepare the second helper or interceptor coming from the opposite side to rotate fast.

Coaches can use progression drills in the Team Build-Up and Game Simulation section on the practice plan to start with 3v3, 4v4, and 5v5 shell defense and always convert it into a live situation.

For example, during practice, have three offensive players, one at the top of the key and the other two at each of the wings. Once 01 passes 02 to the right side, X1 will fly to trap 02. The opposite X3 will shift to the middle to block the 01 open lanes to the basket. The offensive players will not cut through at the moment. The offense will hold the ball for 2 seconds and pass it back to safety at the top. The offense will repeat the process of passing to the left wing to make the defense proactive in shifting to adjust position and be ready to trap.

Then, the coach can add another element: a fourth player in offense and defense to implement traps. The spacing between the four needs to be modified as the player swings the ball, and the mimic continues. This fourth player can be anybody; it is to drill how to help the trapper by shifting to the middle. The fourth defensive player on the opposite side will be splitting two players once the trap begins.

Players can mimic moving on time to modify their positioning and close the open lanes to the basket as much as possible. The coach will command the offensive players at the wing that they can skip the ball to force abrupt rotations.

Once the players have the opportunity to trap, help, and switch, the coach can increase the difficulty by adding cuts from the passer and finding ways to switch out to keep your defensive balance. The coach can make disadvantage drills such as 4v3 shell defense without traps but with skips and ball reversals.

For example, suppose the coach wants to use only three players in defense intentionally and four in offense to create a mismatch. In that case, the coach can command the wing player to skip the pass to force them to compensate in the rotation and assess their communication, readability, and reaction. After the challenge section, the coach can add the fifth player when they play live trap and rotations. The fifth player, who can be a big man, must go out to the corner and close. There are many drills and variations to the shell drill defense. Still, the objective here is to give you an overview of the basic progressions viable to practice a proactive and functional defense when setting traps. There are many variables when it comes to compensating in traps, switches, or recovering, and it depends on assessing your defensive capabilities and the offenses.

UPWARD TRAPS

Another way of trapping in a zone is if X2 can trap 01 from the same side, coming upwards when the zone has a top player like 1-2-2 or using two players at the top like the 2-2-1 zone formation. Trapping from the same side in a 1-2-2 requires an agile shooting guard or small forward to come higher to intercept the ball as the second help. The same side trapper is recommended in the zone if the ball handler just chose a side or was forced to define aside. It causes a player to make a lob pass once they perceive the trap is coming, and the receiver can't move until the ball gets to their hand (Normally, players aware of the ball tend to freeze). It gives the defender a chance the steal. The problem here can be if the trap comes from the small forward side. This can compromise the center, which is supposed to be a safety to go outside to help the corner contest a possible shot.

FUNNEL TRAPS

In zone funnels traps or 'lanes' (The left and right lane at full-court), you can set traps by sending the offensive player to dribble to the sides. You will trap in the pocket areas that are the corners of the half-court of the offensive team. Here we trap going north-south. The player chasing behind the ball handler will go to flip the ball from behind. At the same time, there are still offensive players in the defense's area on the backcourt. It forces the player to play forward towards the basket only. The player will not have the chance to pass back to safety because it will be a backcourt violation. It happens at full-court, but the same principle applies to half-court trapping on the corners on the straight lines of the zone. For example, in a 1-2-2 zone defense, the 01 player passes to 02 at the wing. As soon as 02 swings it to 04 at the corner, X1 will relay the X2 zone player, so X2 can fly with the ball to help X4 trap 04 at the corner. In this scenario, X1 must sag down and switch their zone to cover the X2 zone on time. This timing needs to be drilled in different live scenarios at practice.

FLAT TRAPS

The flat traps come from the two players at the top of the zone. It induces the guard to go middle instead of the triangle mentioned above. It can be executed using zones 2-3, 2-2-1, and 2-1-2. Let's say, for example, the 01, as soon as they pass the half-court. Relatively 01 is staying in the center (Not choosing an extreme side). The top two defensive players will aggressively go to trap to force a desperate lob pass from the ball handler. The other two interceptors need to shift up to reduce the passer's court visibility. This makes them undecided about the pass, but your team must contain the temptation to go for the steal unless the game situation requires taking the risk to steal it.

There are some underlying principles when playing a proactive defense and setting traps. For example, if guard 01 chooses an extreme right side passing half-court and perceives the flat trap is coming, it will make the X2 left side (opposite) travel more distance to help. The problem is that the chances to steal here are low because 01 increased court space, making 02 relocate higher as safety. The X4 will confront a dilemma whether to go for the steal or let the 02 receive the ball. Coaches can send a player to the middle if the team has a tall good passer or any good passer. Then, you may modify the zone to provide a middle person, such as the 2-1-2, to protect you from that middle pass. A middle pass causes many problems on the defense as it can confuse your defense and generate backdoors.

In the scenario presented, the defensive team is in a lose-lose situation if the offense utilizes more space and uses a middle person who is a good passer. But, if the defense induces player 01 to stay in the center, you are more in control of your court coverage. Therefore, the trap can have a higher success probability. The opposite 04 interceptor can assess whether to go for the steal if the distance is at least three long steps of separation from the 02 or just to contain in a ready stance. This separation falls within the accepted marker to risk the steal. If your team doesn't get the steal, the distance to recover back and rotate successfully is more feasible.

I recommend using two levels of risk assessment to increase advantages or minimize disadvantages.

The level of risk are:

- **Level Two: Unnecessary** - this risk is one we want to avoid. It can be an injury risk, wasting energy, putting a big guy in a mismatch situation, or having a guard defending the post.

- **Level One: Necessary** - this is the risk you can use as 'negotiation.' You have to give away something to increase the chance of winning or taking advantage. For example, it can risk leaving the opposite small forward open to use its defender to close more driving and passing lanes. On the other hand, it can be letting the big guy receive the ball in a zone when flashes by the free-throw line and allowing them take most shots. The level of assessment will help you or your players assess the situation better and identify if the benefits are far greater than the risks. Players learn differently, and you want to give them as many tools as possible to become successful. I found four major capability traits and characteristics that help players process information and execute effectively. These traits can make a person become a successful basketball player.

1. Players with high basketball IQ may listen to the general idea. Then, they execute applying more details the right way. They make connections and fill the gaps more consistently.
2. Players with low basketball IQ may not process information fast or have a problem understanding but execute effectively by specific commands from the coach in the most given scenario.
3. Players who perform well by physical ability (speed, strength, height, leaping capabilities); if they have low basketball IQ or experience, they can still be productive and essential to the team. However, if, in addition, they have a solid basketball IQ or expertise, the player may be an NBA star prospect.
4. 'Hybrid players' with multiple capabilities may have some knowledge of the game. They can reflect the predominance of one or various traits mentioned above and effectively do a little of everything.

DIVERSITY AT-A-GLANCE

The beauty of basketball is its diversity —the variety in skills, learning capabilities, personalitites, knowledge, and backgrounds. As a coach, you have the opportunity to build a team using this diversity to form a functional basketball team or transform a chaotic team into a functional and exemplary successful team. Coaches need to inquire more about their demographics. It is possible by speaking about interests and goals, grades and limitations.

In a professional setting, administrators can administer a psychological test to players. This will help to understand the player accurately, integrate them successfully into the team and help them cope with the team's personality. This way, you can identify their needs and significant learning traits to provide them with the means to develop a functional team. It is essential to create this profile of players, not to prejudice or stigmatize them, to reasonably seek a way to establish your philosophy based on your team's personality and differentiate instruction that will successfully support the individual and their success as a team member.

However, as a school coach, professional, or travel team, you will not always be able to implement your philosophy if you inherited players and did not form them, and the time factor is against you to have them buy in into your coaching beliefs. Indeed, they may not successfully run your game-like style. However, adjust your preferences for the more significant benefit of the team. You will ensure your team's success.

DIAGONAL TRAP

The diagonal trap is helpful to trap the post or use the middle player in the zone to trap the wings or corners using that middle player in the zone. For example, a 2-1-2 and a 1-3-1 help you use the middle player to surprise diagonally to trap in or out of the paint. The middle player can be a versatile small forward and get to the trap on time. Then the coach sets norms of who is dropping to protect the middle. Regularly, it is the opposite wing that drops middle. Here, the weakness is the distance going to trap, but it can give you the surprise element to your advantage. An excellent way to propose this tactic is when you intend to show a 'fake' 1-3-1 zone and convert it into a 2-3 to trap at the wings. Just make sure to drill this and have the right players in the zone. The moment the small forward goes to trap at the wing, the center will still protect the middle, and the small forward at the opposite wing will sag to protect the aggressive 2-3 zone.

PRINCIPLE 53: ROTATING OPTIONS

There are different ways to have your players rotate. Choosing the proper rotation depends on your team's ability to process information and execute quickly. Also, it depends on the opponent's advantage against your teams, such as speed, distance, height, passing, dribbling skills, and maturity.

Some coaches teach one rotation to keep it simple. This keeps the same idea intact to help the players execute the same thing to avoid confusion. Some do this intentionally because it may be the best way to have their players in the same mindset. Others, in reality, don't speak about this in detail. However, if you only choose one way to teach, it is okay if the objective at hand is winning. Still, if you are developing, we must teach the players these options and give them the opportunity of judgement when the game situation is presented. Players deserve the rigor and the challenge to become independent in their reasoning. The choices they make on the court can be reflected in their daily life situations and the extent of its success is how you approach and impact their life as the role model coach. Here are some ideas for different rotations, such as same-side rotation, opposite rotation, and big guy help and rotation.

SAME SIDE ROTATION

Rotating the same side is the go-to first option once your team is at a disadvantage by a short distance of at least four long steps or less. For example, if the player X1 is left behind by 01 and X1 can't catch up, but they keep chasing the back of the attacker while X2 closes the driving lane of 01, then X1 can do *'relay defense'* with X2. X2 will try to help stop and recover once X1 has caught up with their player 01. Another option regularly will be to switch (X1 to X2). It will be if they perceive the 01 will penetrate the barrier of your defense toward the basket with the momentum. Then X1 will immediately sprint to switch to the same side to help the X2 helper cover the 02 wing left alone and possibly intercept the extra pass from 01. There are some parameters for making rotations in man-to-man and zones, but the principles are generally the same.

Your player X1 will stay rotating on the same side and avoid switching at first with X2. However, when an offensive player is beating your X1 player, and they are not catching up, have X1 desist chasing and switch with X2 to cover 02 at the right-wing. On the other hand, suppose your player X1 gets beaten easily. For example, the player is left behind in transition or a drive-and-kick against a zone. Then, you will automatically have your players rotate opposite because somebody from the ball side has to turn towards the ball to contain it, creating a chain reaction. You don't want to break it as it makes more variables and increases errors.

However, chaos will happen. As much as we want to control variables to have certainty, it won't always happen. Players must have the individual judgement to 'fill in' the gaps by principles. If players compensate for a matchup, they will do so with the principles already taught to them, and they can successfully overcome the situation.

Opposite Rotation

Let's say, for example, a guard attacks from the top of the key to the right side of the lane-line by the free-throw line, close to the elbow. It will draw the help of defense X2 from the wing. This situation would compromise the help defense X2 to close the driving lane if the X1 guard got beaten or left behind. It could mean that 01 leaves behind the guard X1 going to the right side of the court, moving counterclockwise, it forces the next player from the wing to help on defense clockwise. But since the help defense is leaving their man or zone to help by going clockwise, it means that somebody in offense is left alone on the opposite side. Here, the X1 player left behind by four or more distance steps needs to sprint clockwise to help the guard defensive player who dropped in a man and ball stance to cover the open offensive player that is probably by the corner. The opposite rotation is triggered by the distance to recover to catch the 01 guards who took advantage of your X1. Ideally, we want to avoid unnecessary risks, like involving all the players in the rotation, as it increases the chance of confusion and mismatch and requires more communication and team effort. We want to avoid this and first try the same side rotations and add the switch if necessary. It can help when guards are trying to match in transition. They must **level their defense** instead of going forward and trying to steal the ball. They assess the speed and realize how the player will reduce the ball handler's speed and space by inducing the direction to the help or 'crowd' and meeting into a midpoint to matchup in the same conditions.

BIG GUY HELP AND ROTATION

Scenario one-same side: a **double offensive tag** on the right side of the half-court. 02 is at the wing, and 04 goes to the corner after posting for a couple of seconds, the 03 player is on the opposite left wing as a single tag, and the 05 player is close to the block on the left side. The guard 01 from the top of the key, trying to the fake going left side, will spin and turn to the right side with momentum to attack through the right side between the lane line and wing, getting close to the paint. While 01 is beating X1, the X2 wing can only 'stunt' the penetrator but cannot leave 02 because the player is a sharpshooter. In this case, we will keep the perspective that 04 at the corner has a lower three-point percentage. Therefore, we will use their defender X4 to help intercept the driving lane of 01 by dropping close to the block. Once X4 is closing out on 01, X1 that was delayed chasing 01 will be alert to sprint to the corner to cover 04 and contest a possible shot. The X2 can sag and play decent defense, ready to help at the corner (just in an emergency) until X1 recovers to 04 at the corner. If the X2 decides to help the corner to close on 04, X1 runs towards the 02 instead of the corner. However, it is risky because the sharpshooter is left unguarded for an instant, and X1 must turn to locate the shooter. Therefore, the sharpshooter could move intelligently to increase their advantage. The triple rotation occurs when X4 must step to close out on 01 due to X1 not stopping 01 from penetrating, and a breach on your defense is forced to compensate abruptly.

Scenario two-skip pass: Suppose the ball is kicked out from the 01 to the left side, where the 03 and the 05 are. The splitting X3 was low to intercept the possible dish pass to the 05 while the X5 was in the help position on the mid-right side. If the pass goes to the 03 wing, the X3 must be ready to sprint to close out on wing 03, and X5 returns to match 05. On the other hand, if the pass goes to 05 as a dish, the 03 wingmen will be left alone because X3 is dropping to intercept the possible pass to 05, and X1 must identify it and sprint out to closeout on 03. After two help rotations, players on the weak side must be trying to recover to help appropriately, not just having their backs turned and becoming spectators.

Scenario three-opposite side: If there is no offensive 04 player on the right side at the corner, and there is just **one single-tag** at the wing, which is the shooter 02, and intentionally is increasing court space by dropping to the corner, it will force the rotation to go in the opposite-direction (clockwise). It will be caused by where the help comes from. For example, the X2 defender just 'stunts' to fake that they will close the driving lane of 01 and return to their corner 02 player.

If the big X5 is compromised, closing on the 01, the X4 player, who may be close to the opposite left short corner, will help cover 05. Then, wing X3 may rotate or sag down to the mid-post area by the short corner to cover 04. The guard X1 left behind will rotate opposite 'clockwise' to cover the 03 outer men to the opposite wing.

Many Times in zone, when the guard makes a way through the middle and the big guy is compromised, the offensive guard will kick out. Then, you want to have your guards ready to contest the three-pointers instead of chasing the back of the attacker. When it happens, guards regularly stop chasing, watching the big guy helping, and are not ready to close out on the perimeter when there is a kick out. Also, do your best not to allow middle penetrations to compromise the big for a foul. It will be hard for your players to define where the help defense will come from, bigs are compromised, and dishes are deadly. It is a situation that might put your team at a disadvantage if it is not well drilled at practice and there is no team communication.

PRINCIPLE 54: HAVE DESIGNATED SAFETY DEFENSIVE PLAYERS

What does safety defense mean? The coach designates a safety defensive player to protect the paint from any fast breaks and when there are traps that create mismatches.

In defense, you need somebody to protect the paint if you are pressing. Regularly, it is the big guy who stays, but it doesn't have to be that way. You can designate who will be the safety man, given the scenario. Suppose you have an agile, strong forward player, and the opposite team has small players on the court. Then play man-to-man and switch mainly with everybody if the need arises, but have the last man in the rotation sag close to the paint as safety. Your big man doesn't have to stay in the paint, but the last man who drops to be a safety will play between two players, especially if your team traps and there will be a mismatch. However, you will still need a safety player if pressing full man-to-man court after a dead ball. You designate a player not to chase their player and leave the paint unprotected. Set expectations or remind the player about this. Give them the judgement opportunity of how far they must follow the player.

Remember, staying in a triangular stance close to the epicenter of the paint to protect the basket is the most generally accepted practice.

For instance, if you have a center playing against a small forward and often forces your center to come out of the paint, designate zone coverages for both of your bigs. Tell your center to always stay in the paint as a safety. The strong forward can defend whoever is out of the paint with more speed advantage over your center. This way, you ensure that your center doesn't create a disadvantage by stepping out, but you have the best defender staying in the paint.

GREAT OFFENSE = BETTER DEFENSE

Concentrate on your offense's decision-making to ensure your defense will have a greater chance of success. This can affect how well your team will defend transitions and fast breaks. For example, a standard shooting philosophy is that if you are open, then 'shoot it'! The problem is that, as I mentioned before, what about if everyone considers themselves open? And who is your player left open to take most of the shots?

Also, consider that long-range shots have a lower percentage of effectiveness. It suggests a greater chance that the ball missed will make a longer bounce or bounce off the paint. Therefore, it will be advantageous for the opposite team to begin the fastbreak with an outlet pass. When your team is attacking, you will need to have the opposite man from the wing rotating higher to stay as a safety transition defender in case of an interception.

Also, from a rebounding standpoint, try to put your best rebounder opposite the shooters or make them go opposite after a shot. It will increase the chance of the team getting the possession and decrease the risk of giving a second chance to the opponent. Coaches must designate roles in this matter and always create awareness that the most important thing is to protect the basket and limit the offensive second chance possessions. Illustrate that they can't just jump to contest a shot in a fast break or gamble to steal the ball. This leaves the offensive player a complete driving lane to the basket when there is no one to help.

Suppose your team is aware and conscious of the value of making the right offensive decisions, such as shooting, passing, and relocating. In that case, it will facilitate defensive transitioning, increasing your defensive system's success rate. That's the intrinsic value of your offense, and it helps your defensive players reduce fouls rate, injuries, moral implications, team conflict, and unnecessary drama, which makes your experience more pleasant. In addition, it will allow you to focus on improving and innovating. But if you are caught frequently in team conflicts triggered by defensive misalignments, the growth you know you can create may be faded from common team controversies. As you know, inequitable shooting and defensive opportunities, parents' unbalanced high expectations, and defensive misconceptions are the principal elements affecting team morale.

PRINCIPLE 55: LEVERAGING RISKS AND GAMBLING

Learning from intentional or unintentional mistakes is also part of being proactive. There must be a learning opportunity in everything experienced in the game. Some risks are necessary to step out of the comfort zone, learn from the experiment, and positively contribute to the basketball game and the player's life. We must intentionally take measured risks and learn from the adverse results or the success obtained.

I understand that there is so much pride, and taking risks is something not accepted by many basketball commentators. It may be seen as a dumb mistake on your part. You may feel pressured to coach the way is generally accepted. However, you must innovate and constantly seek ways to improve to impact the game and players' lives. You will experience a positive evolution of basketball in your area that will benefit many, even if you don't get the credit. Still, it will be a great learning opportunity and a rewarding experience. It has happened to me multiple times, but this reminds me of the following quote:

"When the best leader's work is done, the people say, 'we' did it ourselves." - Lao Tzu

What truly matters is the cause of what you are doing, not your benefit. However, I am sharing some of the controlled team risks you can take considering the landmark of time, score, and a quarter during the game:

1. Risk to trap
2. Risk to press
3. Risk to steal
4. Risk to go zone
5. Risk to go man to man
6. Risk to play slow half-court
7. Risk of switching everything
8. Risk to leave a man open
9. Risk of mirroring the opponent

Any decision to change the 'defensive look' involves a certain level of risk since many variable 'pros' suggest the defensive strategy change in your favor. Still, there are also 'cons' indicating that the change may have adverse effects. However, it is something that you must leverage and decide whether to risk it or not. Let's use point 9, 'mirroring the opponent,' as an example. If you fall behind on the score in the game and cannot control the variables to your favor, try to seek leverage by mirroring the opponent's strategies to lower their morale. It induces them to fight from within to force them to play individually by the anarchy created. Although we may employ this principle at high school levels and above, we don't want to use this with lower levels for different reasons. For example, suppose you surprise the team as they most likely have not prepared a scouting strategy to play against their tactics since they have focused on beating the opponent's strategy. The surprise element can help you level the scoreboard and give you another winning chance or, at least, a decent comeback. By mirroring what the opponent is doing right and effectively, you may be surprised how your player can model the opponent's example.

You can risk using this tactic when you see that what you have practiced is not working, the team's energy seems low, and team morale is critical. The risk is that the team has practiced their tactics. Sometimes, however, they use a tactic they did not practice but just got into without planning. If you mimic what they are doing right, it gives you a chance to have leverage and force the winning team to step out from their winning strategies. For example, press if they are pressing and you are not. It will exhaust them and may lower their shooting percentage. If they have success playing 1-3-1 zone, then go 1-3-1 zone and copy what makes it a success.

I've realized that copying the same tactics during a bad game for your team will force the other team to drop what is working and improvise if what you copy is working against them. They will get distracted and may get frustrated. Once you do that, you push the team to fight from within and divide themselves into subgroups. Coaches will make desperate subs, dropping morale. Here you are using the art of confusion.

Disclaimer: Do not apply this in youth basketball; only use this tactic if winning is critical and at all costs for higher-level competition.

Remember, as long as there is a shot clock, maximize your team's efficiency and opportunities. Risks are always involved. When you are trying to catch up, you can gamble, go for the steals, and trap more consistently. You can also press more or change the looks of the defense. Alternatively, try to increase the team foul after half of the fourth quarter, then start fouling with reasonable time to their lower percentage free-throw shooting player.

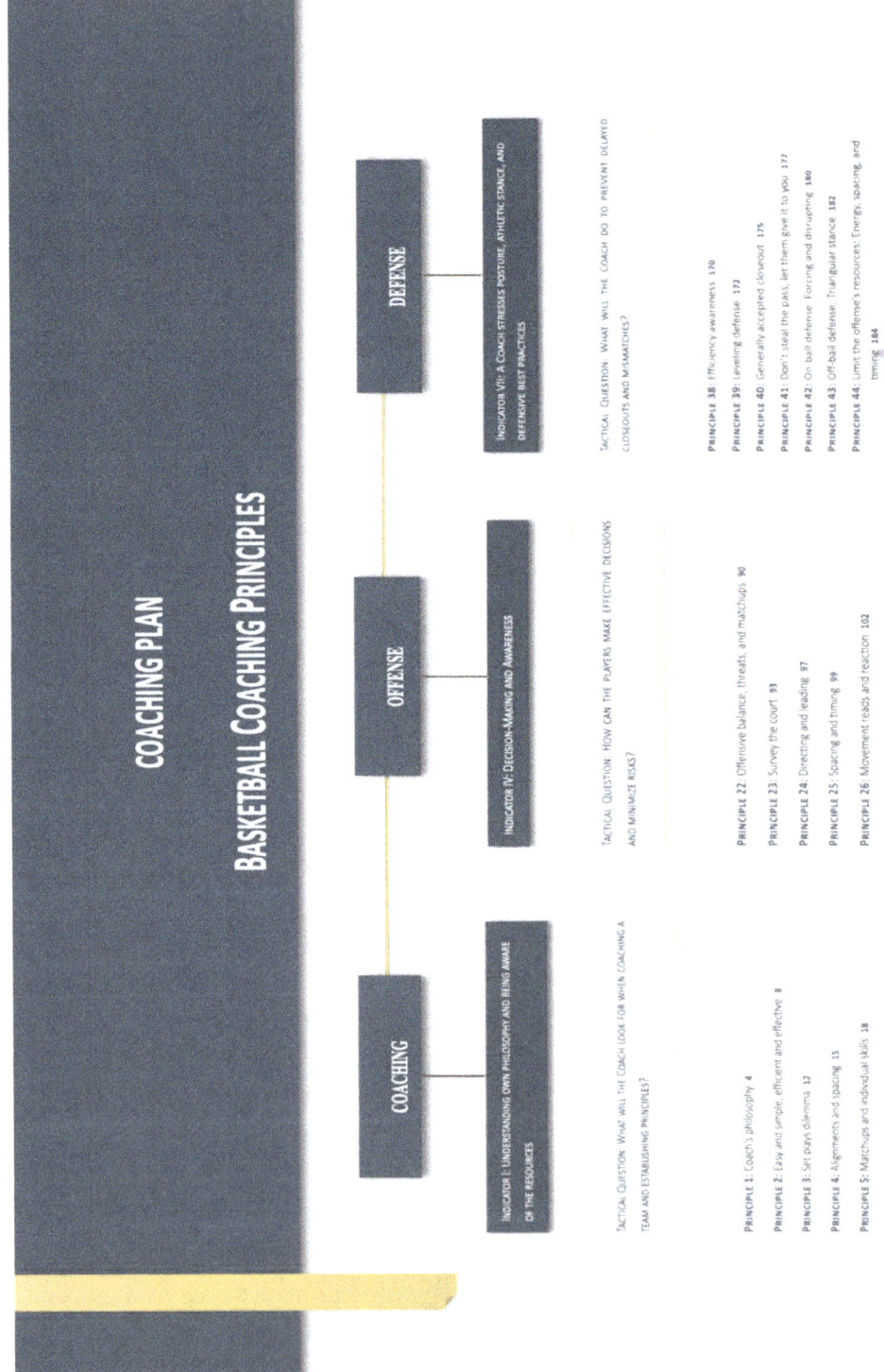

COACHING PLAN

BASKETBALL COACHING PRINCIPLES

COACHING

INDICATOR I: UNDERSTANDING OWN PHILOSOPHY AND BEING AWARE OF THE RESOURCES

TACTICAL QUESTION: WHAT WILL THE COACH LOOK FOR WHEN COACHING A TEAM AND ESTABLISHING PRINCIPLES?

PRINCIPLE 1: Coach's philosophy 4

PRINCIPLE 2: Easy and simple, efficient and effective 8

PRINCIPLE 3: Set plays dilemma 12

PRINCIPLE 4: Alignments and spacing 15

PRINCIPLE 5: Matchups and individual skills 18

OFFENSE

INDICATOR IV: DECISION-MAKING AND AWARENESS

TACTICAL QUESTION: HOW CAN THE PLAYERS MAKE EFFECTIVE DECISIONS AND MINIMIZE RISKS?

PRINCIPLE 22: Offensive balance, threats, and matchups 90

PRINCIPLE 23: Survey the court 93

PRINCIPLE 24: Directing and leading 97

PRINCIPLE 25: Spacing and timing 99

PRINCIPLE 26: Movement reads and reaction 102

DEFENSE

INDICATOR VII: A COACH STRESSES POSTURE, ATHLETIC STANCE, AND DEFENSIVE BEST PRACTICES

TACTICAL QUESTION: WHAT WILL THE COACH DO TO PREVENT DELAYED CLOSEOUTS AND MISMATCHES?

PRINCIPLE 38: Efficiency awareness 170

PRINCIPLE 39: Leveling defense 173

PRINCIPLE 40: Generally accepted closeout 175

PRINCIPLE 41: Don't steal the pass, let them give it to you 177

PRINCIPLE 42: On ball defense. Forcing and disrupting 180

PRINCIPLE 43: Off ball defense. Triangular stance 182

PRINCIPLE 44: Limit the offense's resources: Energy, spacing, and timing 184

| Coaching   Principles |

www.ingramcontent.com/pod-product-compliance
Lightning Source LLC
Chambersburg PA
CBHW060912120626
46553CB00001B/301

* 9 7 9 8 2 1 8 0 3 1 1 6 9 *